We Built a Village

We Built a Village

Cohousing and the Commons

Diane Rothbard Margolis

Foreword by David Bollier

New Village Press • New York

Published in the United States by New Village Press

bookorders@newvillagepress.net
www.newvillagepress.org

New Village Press is a public-benefit, nonprofit publisher

Distributed by NYU Press

Publication Date: August 23, 2022

First Edition

Paperback 9781613321782
Hardcover 9781613321799
eBook 9781613321805

Library of Congress Cataloging-in-Publication Data
available online at http://catalog.loc.gov

Cover photo: Raines Cohen
Cover design: Lynne Elizabeth
Interior design and composition: Leigh McLellan Design

The names of many individuals in this memoir have
been changed to protect their privacy.

For My Fellow Cohousers at
Cambridge Cohousing

Also by Diane Rothbard Margolis

The Managers: Corporate Life in America

The Fabric of Self: A Theory of Ethics and Emotions

Contents

Foreword

by David Bollier

The art of commoning, while not always easy, opens up compelling new solutions for many significant challenges. This should not be surprising. Commoning has been the default mode of human social organization for millennia. It's only been over the past two centuries, with the rise of industrial capitalism, that humanity's connections to earthly systems, one another, and collective purposes have atrophied.

For Americans accustomed to a culture of radical individualism and market norms, the very idea of commoning may seem discomfiting. Can we come to recognize the new vistas of possibility that cooperation, sharing, mutual aid, and the pooling of our wealth can provide? Can we begin to see the constructive new energies and social emancipation, the sense of belonging, connection, and place-based identity, that commoning engenders?

Diane Margolis probes these and many other themes as she recounts her adventures in cohousing. In the early 1990s, following the death of her husband, she embarked upon a quest to start one of the earliest cohousing projects in the United States. Cambridge

Cohousing, in Cambridge, Massachusetts, was a bold, experimental gambit at a time when there were few cohousing projects to study and emulate. (Now there are more than three hundred in the United States.)

Countless questions and challenges arose: How does one convene a diverse set of strangers to become long-term commoners and neighbors? How can people find ways to bring their diverse financial interests and needs into alignment? What is the process by which one's individual wants are reconciled with collective needs? How do forty families living in the same residential complex come to govern themselves and their building well?

We Built a Village, Margolis's lively account of Cambridge Cohousing's birth and development, not only addresses these questions, it points to some larger lessons for our time. Instead of looking simply to markets or the state for answers, we need to see that peer-organized commons offer many compelling alternatives of their own. There are many things we can do ourselves, together, as commoners, right now. Moreover, the character of our peer governance and provisioning will reflect levels of care, trust, and social sensitivity that the market/state system cannot provide.

But commoning is not simply about meeting our material needs. It's equally about people growing together. It's about our inner development as humans. As the farmer/philosopher Wendell Berry has written, "Only the purpose of a coherent community, fully alive both in the world and in the minds of its members, can carry us beyond fragmentation, contradiction, and negativity, teaching us to preserve, not in opposition but in affirmation and affection, all things needful to make us glad to live."

We Built a Village is an engaging story of one group of spirited commoners who found great satisfaction and success in relying on one another. This book shows how you, too, can embark upon a similar journey.

David Bollier

David Bollier, a longtime commons scholar and activist, directs the Reinventing the Commons Program at the Schumacher Center for a New Economics. He is an author or editor of eight books on the commons, including (with Silke Helfrich) *Free, Fair, and Alive* (2019) and *The Commoner's Catalog for Changemaking* (2021). He blogs at Bollier.org and lives in Amherst, Massachusetts.

Preface

We're All in This Together
The Call of the Commons

In 2020, the world was attacked by COVID-19; the month of May saw SpaceX become the first private company to launch astronauts into our galactic common spaces; and in autumn, severe thunderstorms ignited wildfires across the West Coast of the United States. Now, as the world struggles to reopen, the virus forces retreat in jurisdictions that didn't protect their commons with universal vaccinations. A more dramatic demonstration of the power and importance of commons is hard to imagine—the pandemic may turn out to be the wake-up call the world needs to force us to recognize our many commons and our need to protect them. My country and the world are at a turning point that makes this book's purpose clear: It is the story of some fifty strangers coming together to build their homes and their community, a commons. It will help us explore the differences between markets and commons in everyday terms. When we know those differences, perhaps enough of us will give to commons the care and attention we now bestow on commodities and markets—thereby we may save our planet.

Commons is a term familiar to historians, lawyers, anthropologists, and activists. Jonathan Rowe, a journalist who was among the first to note the value of commons and the danger they were in, wrote:

> The commons includes our entire life support system, both natural and social. The air and the oceans, the web of species, wilderness and flowing water—all are parts of the commons. So are language and knowledge, sidewalks and public squares, stories of childhoods, the processes of democracy. Some parts of the commons are gifts of nature, others the product of human endeavor. Some are new, such as the Internet; others are as ancient as soil and calligraphy. (Rowe 2013, 14)

Commons are ubiquitous and, like the air we breathe, largely invisible. Commons are everything a group of people owns and uses together, from its water systems or fishing grounds to its language and its culture. The Earth and the universe are commons. A commons is not a commodity, and although some enterprising shysters are selling deeds to the moon, a commons cannot be bought or sold, for as soon as it is, it becomes a commodity.

Commons go back to prehistoric times, when protohumans and humans treated the whole Earth as a commons. Whatever there was, was there for the taking. By the time the Romans had taken control of a corner of the Earth, things had become more complicated, so they developed a codification scheme. Property that could be possessed by an individual or family, such as a home and its furnishings, they called res privata; things held in common by many people and managed by the state—for example, parks, roads, harbors, and ports—they called res publica; things open to all by their nature, such as the oceans and the air, they called res communes; and property belonging to a group, such as guilds, merchant groups, New York City in its early days, and what today we call a commons, the Romans called res universitatis (Rose 2003).

The Magna Carta granted areas called the commons to the common people for specified purposes, such as cutting wood, hunting, gathering honey, or fishing. The commons helped to support the commoners until the nineteenth century, when the utilization of the power loom vastly increased the market for wool and the rich and powerful passed many enclosure laws and fenced the commons. Often the commoners were promised some recompense for their loss. Then "the Lord will provide" took on a new and sinister meaning, because the lord of the manor was usually not a good provider and commoners were forced into cities to sell their only possession, their labor.

We may now be coming to the end of an era when markets dominate economic life and entering a time when we will question the wisdom, maybe even the possibility, of turning everything into commodities. Maybe we will wake up to our dwindling commons and understand that without commons there can be no life on Earth, and that without commons, commodities will be worthless.

At the beginning of the Industrial Revolution, when markets were becoming a predominant form of economic life, commons were so abundant that one could abuse them with impunity. Now we must take care; all over our planet, we are experiencing the effects of climate change. The air we breathe is becoming unbreathable; soon it won't be there just for the inhaling. Asthma increases, children need inhalers, and we approach public places wearing masks.

We act differently when we are in a commons from how we act in a market; when we are contributing our labor and our skills rather than selling them; when we are sharing our gifts and insights rather than patenting them and turning them into commodities. Our values, what we consider good and just, are different when they guide us in commons from when they guide us in markets.

In the pages that follow, we will watch and listen as the fifty or so people who came together to build Cambridge Cohousing used everyday language to discuss these differences and to decide whether something would be a commodity or a commons. For they were simultaneously building their homes—for most of them, their most valuable private property—and their community, their commons.

It would be a mistake to think of the commons and the market as opposites or opposing value systems; they are, in fact, the warp and weft of contemporary life. Woven together, they make life possible. As in any fabric, the warp, like the commons, is primary, basic, the frame or basis on which the weft is woven to create the fabric of life.

Introduction

Nineteen ninety-one was a watershed year. It brought the fall of the Soviet Union and ushered in what one writer called "market triumphalism" and another "the second enclosure," both deploring the transfer of common goods to private ownership (Sandel 2012; Boyle 2003, 43). Working in the opposite direction and making a major contribution to the commons, Tim Berners-Lee launched the World Wide Web with the core principle that everyone should be able to communicate freely with everyone else (Berners-Lee 2000). Along with those changes and largely because of them, individualism continued its century-long march, eclipsing community and forcing people young and old to feel isolated and so lonely that in 2018 the prime minister of Great Britain established a ministry of loneliness (see https://www.nytimes.com/2018/01/17/world/europe/uk-britain-loneliness.html) and the surgeon general of the United States declared that the country was suffering a loneliness epidemic (see https://www.washingtonpost.com/news/on-leadership/wp/2017/10/04/this-former-surgeon-general-says-theres-a-loneliness-epidemic-and-work-is-partly-to-blame/).

Nineteen ninety-one was also the year my husband died and I began the journey that led me to help found Cambridge Cohousing and, in the process, to discover the connections between market triumphalism and loneliness on the one hand and the commons on the other.

When Dick died, my private world crumbled. Our friends gathered around me for a while, and then I was alone and isolated. I watched the news and knew that in other parts of the world, women, along with their daughters, were being raped, their husbands, sons, and brothers murdered before their eyes. I wondered how they kept going and was embarrassed to feel sorry for myself. Even without Dick, I had so much. As a white citizen of a rich and powerful nation, I was safe. I had friends, a professorship in my chosen field of sociology, enough money to put whatever I wanted on the table, and two sons who had flown the coop and were doing well.

I thanked my grandparents for my good fortune. They were part of the migration of Jews who left Eastern Europe for the United States early in the twentieth century. That put me and all the other immigrants and children of immigrants into a commonwealth that included safe streets, roads and bridges, schools and playgrounds, parks and museums. Even more than that, we enjoyed the intangible benefits of shared values in freedom, liberty, and equality of rights, even if differently situated citizens would enjoy and interpret these benefits differently. They were all benefits that other women lacked as they struggled to stay alive in Rwanda, Croatia, Sierra Leone, Somalia, and dozens of other countries wracked by wars and cruel dictators.

Like my compatriots, I was safe and relatively rich. But I was lonely. As a sociologist, I reflected on a society that focuses as many human needs as ours does on a unit as fragile as the couple. I felt injured by my unwilling entrance into the rising statistic of single-person households and a worldwide epidemic of lonely people.

I read a lot. At the turn of the century, there was a spate of books about isolation in America, including Robert Putnam's popular *Bowling Alone* (2000) and Caroline Knapp's less noticed *Pack of Two* (1998), an exploration into the emotional niches that dogs fill in the lives of their single owners.

I began reading books by widowed authors the way foodies read cookbooks. *A Grief Observed*, by C. S. Lewis, was my favorite in spite of the author's emphasis on faith. (Some of the time I think I'm an atheist; some of the time, annoyed by the religious zeal of some atheists, I'm an agnostic.) I also read books on grief. Kübler-Ross, with her oft-quoted "five stages of grief," put me off until I realized that her theorizing was based on her work with terminally ill patients and analyzes the process people go through when they are told they are close to death or about to lose some body part. She wasn't really theorizing about mourning the love of your life. Now there are many more books by widows and widowers. Two of these describe their authors' first years of widowhood. The more famous is Joan Didion's *Year of Magical Thinking* (2005); the one that better reflects my experience is Anne Roiphe's *Epilogue* (2008). Three pages from the end of her book, Roiphe writes:

> What I would like is a summer camp for adults my age, with a communal dining room and taps at night and weekly movies and campfires and songs. . . . But such a place if it existed would be filled with the near-blind, the hardly hearing, the limping, the sad, the lonely, the diseased, or about to be diseased. It would be hard to keep up one's courage there. . . . A summer camp that never ends is not such a good idea. (Roiphe 2008, 211)

My own dream was not of a summer camp that never ends, but of a writers and artists colony where you could go whenever you wanted, and stay for as long as you wished. When Dick died, Harriet Barlow, the director of Blue Mountain Center, a colony in the Adirondacks, where Dick and I had enjoyed several residencies, offered me Dick's residency for that June. I welcomed the chance to return there.

What I most wanted were the dinners where the artists and writers gather every evening after a solitary day's work in their studios. Widowed people often find themselves loneliest at a particular time of day. Some are reminded of their loss upon waking up to an empty bed, others as they slide between the icy sheets at the end of the day. For me, dinnertime was the loneliest time of the day. Perhaps that was because dinnertime had been the best of times.

Two images come to mind. One was of the Three Bears Restaurant in Westport, Connecticut, where we would go for an occasional dinner out. When our waitress came with our bill one evening, she said, "I loved watching you; most couples hardly talk to each other, but you two never stopped." I was surprised. Even after thirty-seven years, our marriage was a nonstop conversation. I thought all marriages were like that.

My other memory was of something that happened once or twice a week for years. I'd come home to our Queen Anne Victorian on Bishop Street in New Haven, park our Honda in the driveway by the side of our house, let myself in, and start up the stairs to our apartment on the second and third floors. As I'd turn the bend onto the second floor, Dick would be there smiling, obviously delighted to see me. We'd kiss, and he'd take my briefcase in one hand and wrap me in a big bear hug with the other arm as we took the last steps into our dining room, where he had set the table, complete with lighted candles. It was nothing unusual. When Dick prepared dinner, which he did on the days I went in to teach, he often made a celebration of it.

Soon after those celebrations ended, I began talking to friends about forming a dinner club, some plan whereby we'd have dinner together at each other's houses or at restaurants on some regular basis without the bother of invitations and special arrangements. At first that idea looked as though it was going to be about as successful as an earlier plan I had when our children were youngsters. I called it "The Liberation Floor Plan." As a wife and mother in the early days of the women's movement, I added up the meals I cooked each year and the hours I spent driving kids to this lesson and that game. It seemed a waste of time and energy to do it all alone. I thought that less suburban privacy and more communal cooperation could leave time for other pursuits. Not yet a sociologist at the time, but thinking about becoming an architect or city planner, I was a reader of utopias such as Edward Bellamy's *Looking Backward* and Percival and Paul Goodman's *Communitas*, and books with a feminist lens, such as Dolores Hayden's *Redesigning the American Dream*. My Liberation Floor Plan was a circular sort of cooperative dwelling with a common area for the children at the center and parents' more private rooms on the periphery. Housed that way, families, I thought, could cooperate in the care of their children without giving up too much of the privacy we enjoyed on our two-acre suburban plots. I tried to interest friends in my idea and then, having failed to do so, stuffed the plans into a drawer.

Now, faced with a home that was too empty rather than too demanding, I was once again turning to friends and trying to interest them in my dream of a dinner club. That idea was getting no traction, either, but my friends did put me onto another way to dispel loneliness. At a work weekend to get Blue Mountain Center ready for the season, Harriet, the director, said there was something called cohousing, that was similar to what I was talking about. At about the same time, other friends sent me clippings, one from *The New York Times* and one from *The Boston Globe*. They were about cohousing and mentioned a book the cohousing movement calls its "bible": *Cohousing: A Contemporary Approach to Housing Ourselves* by Kathryn McCamant and Charles Durrett. In August 1993, while

I was enjoying a residency at the now defunct Cummington Community for the Arts, I picked up a copy at the nearby Smith College library.

Back in the 1980s, McCamant and Durrett—"Katie" and "Chuck" to folks in the cohousing movement—were a couple of young architects who went to Denmark to look at the *bofaellsskaber* communities that had sprung up in response to the invisible walls separating neighbor from neighbor, which had gotten so high that they would barely exchange the Danish equivalent of "Hi. How are ya?" as they passed on the street. That isolation prompted two Danes to write the newspaper articles that sparked the cohousing movement. One, by the architect Jan Gudmand-Høyer, told about the way his attempt to create the first cohousing community was thwarted by neighbors who feared that "the increased number of children would bring excessive noise to their quiet neighborhood." The other, by Bodil Graae, was titled "Children Should Have One Hundred Parents." Graae complained that "neighborhood design gives greater consideration to cars and parking than to children."

Katie and Chuck were ready to start a family, but, like so many other young couples in the eighties, they worked long hours and had little time to do many of the things that, as a stay-at-home mom, I did in the fifties and sixties—shop, prepare meals, keep house, volunteer and raise money for my local political party and various charities, manage an active social life with invitations and dinner parties several times a month, and, of course, take care of the kids. As Katie and Chuck put it:

> The modern single-family detached home, which makes up
> 67 percent of American housing stock, was designed for a nu-
> clear family consisting of a breadwinning father, a homemaking
> mother, and two to four children. Today, less than one-quarter
> of the United States population lives in such households. Rather,

the family with two working parents predominates, while the single-parent household is the fastest-growing family type. Almost one-quarter of the population lives alone . . . (McCamant and Durrett 1988, 22)

They translated bofaellsskaber as "cohousing" and filled their book with pictures, site plans, floor plans, and descriptions of life in the communities they visited. I was especially taken with the dinners.

"Imagine . . ." they wrote:

It's five o'clock in the evening, and Anne is glad the workday is over. . . . Instead of frantically trying to put together a nutritious dinner, Anne can relax now, spend some time with her children, and then eat with her family in the common house. Walking through the common house on her way home, she stops to chat with the evening's cooks, two of her neighbors, who are busy preparing dinner—broiled chicken with mushroom sauce . . . (McCamant and Durrett 1988, 13)

I was hooked. In some ways, cohousing seemed like a perfect combination of Anne Roiphe's summer camp and my artists and writers colony. It was saved from the stultifying sameness of Roiphe's endless summer camp by the cohousing community's young families with their kids, and it was saved from the short residencies at writers colonies by the fact that most cohousing residents own their homes as condominiums and never have to leave.

My trek to cohousing began that summer. Little did I know then that in my quest for a new kind of home, a home that might protect me from the worst aspects of the coming loneliness pandemic, I would become part of a movement that, as it built this new kind of housing and community, would also be at the forefront of a shift away from market triumphalism and toward a greater concern for the commons. The sustainability movement was already well under way in 1990 and most cohousing communities embraced it. The commons movement, sustainability's sister, still struggles for a foothold in 2021.

One

I Look for a
Cohousing Community

Chuck and Katie's book let me know that I wanted to live in a cohousing community. The question was, how would I find one? In the fall of 1993, there were only seven established cohousing communities in the United States. They were in Colorado, California, and Washington State. None was in Massachusetts, where I wanted to live. Two decades later, in 2014, there would be over 150 cohousing communities in the United States, twelve of them in Massachusetts. There would also be a national organization with a website that included a directory of communities, and a national Listserv where you could announce your wish to find a cohousing group in a particular location and wait for emails to come to you.

But in 1992, the only way I was going to live in a cohousing community in Massachusetts was to help build one. I had to find others who wanted a community and were willing to work for it. An artist at Cummington Center for the Arts, where I was enjoying a residency that summer, was interested. She knew of a group that, in September, would be holding a meeting in Watertown, a town bordering Boston and Cambridge. We agreed to meet there. At the close of the program, I picked up a few flyers and headed back home to Connecticut. I called Steve Hecht, who was mentioned in the Globe article that my friend had sent. He told me about the Cohousing Clearinghouse of Greater Boston (CCGB), which was holding a meeting on September 26. I decided to go.

The room in the Cambridge YWCA was large and bare; hoops at either end said it doubled as a basketball court. As I came in, a few people were putting chairs in a circle. I hesitated by the door, and Stella, a cheery woman in her mid-thirties with a round face and sparkling eyes, came over to me. I told her I was interested in cohousing in the Boston area and that Steve from New View had suggested I come. She said that I had come to the right place. Gently, with her hand on the small of my back, she led me to a table laid out with magazines and flyers. "Look these over while we wait for everybody to get here," she said.

People ambled in. After a few minutes, Stella clapped her hands for attention and asked everybody to take a seat in the circle of chairs at the center of the room. She said a few words about CCGB and then started us off the way most meetings of strangers begin—by asking each of us to give our name and say what brought us there.

As we went around the circle, the second person to speak was Steve. He announced that their group had grown in the past few months from twelve to twenty-two and they were looking for land in Acton, Massachusetts. They wanted more members, especially people over fifty-five. Then a woman from Newton said they were hoping to build a cohousing community with an indoor swimming pool and other upscale amenities. "What about affordability?" someone asked. "That's not one of our goals," the woman from Newton responded somewhat defiantly. I was thinking that Newton was a pretty nice town and an indoor swimming pool sounded just dandy, when the woman from Newton added that they already had everybody they needed; they were a group of friends. Too bad, I thought, just as the man who asked about affordability was saying that her project didn't sound much like cohousing. Stella smiled sweetly and said that each cohousing group had to decide for itself what it was going to be.

There was another group like that: three or four friends trying to get together to form a cohousing community. Then there was a curly-haired, rangy man who sounded more like a New Yorker than I do, and looked straight out of central casting for a guy from the Bronx. He said he was part of a North Shore group made up mostly of health-care professionals that called themselves NorShorCoHo. A woman came from a group centered around the Lexington Waldorf School. They were committed to personal and spiritual growth. A bit too New Age for me, I thought. Another woman, Sandy, said she was part of a group of eight households that wanted to build in Somerville or Cambridge. That sounded better.

In all, there were about fifteen people representing about ten groups and another fifteen looking for a group. When it became Stella's turn to speak again, she said that getting people together, "networking," was what CCGB was all about. As there was no special program that night, she suggested that we get some refreshments and flyers from the tables in the back and just talk with one another. I picked up a bunch of flyers and looked for Sandy. On my way, I overheard a couple of women about my age grumbling about New View's quest for members over fifty-five: "They're just looking for grandmas and free babysitting." Oh no, that's not good, I thought. I wasn't interested in New View anyway. I wanted to live in Boston or Cambridge. I found Sandy. She told me about several groups in the Boston area that she knew about and she promised to let me know about the next meeting she planned to attend. I said I would go if I could. I still had a full-time job teaching sociology at the University of Connecticut; making frequent trips from Connecticut up to Boston was difficult.

Nonetheless, over the next few months I became a member of half a dozen groups and went from meeting to meeting, each one attended mostly by people I never saw again, though I did begin to recognize a few from former meetings, and three would eventually become my neighbors. One was Carla, a tall, divorced woman with two daughters, with whom I formed a short-lived group focused on Cambridge.

Most of the groups trying to form a cohousing community in the Boston area were headed by amateurs like Carla and me, but a few architects were also getting into the act. One headed a group called the Urban Cohousing Study Group. Its first meeting was at this man's house in Cambridge. Fifteen of us showed up. After the usual round of introductions, we went around the room again, this time saying what interested us about cohousing in general and urban cohousing in particular. The responses were common among aspiring cohousers: living in a setting that fostered informal socializing; sharing work; sharing the cost of amenities too expensive for a single owner; having an alternative to traditional, speculative development; and living with a focus on sustainability.

Only four people showed up at their next meeting a couple of weeks later. I wasn't one of them, but I had put myself on the mailing list, so I got the minutes. They weren't encouraging.

> Underlying the discussion was a general sense of disappointment at the low turnout. . . . Cohousing groups, particularly in their formative stage, seem to be long on idealism and short on pragmatism. A discussion of the cost and work involved in the development of cohousing might be more useful at this time than its physical features and spiritual fulfillment. . . . Now is the time to fish or cut bait . . . make every effort to attend the Dec. 7 meeting.

I couldn't get to Cambridge on December 7, either, and I didn't get any more minutes from that group, nor did anything appear in the CCGB newsletter, which in every issue carried a paragraph about each of the groups forming in the Boston area. Like most cohousing groups, the Urban Cohousing Study Group must have died aborning. The odds against any group actually becoming a community are huge. CCGB listed twelve Boston-area cohousing groups in its June 1992 newsletter. Only one came to fruition. In order to gestate successfully, a cohousing group needs many things. At the top of the list is a "burning soul," someone who has the time, the passion, and the energy to stick with a group for the many years—sometimes longer than a decade—that it takes to get from the kind of group that meets two or three times and then disbands to the kind of group that can stick together while it decides where its members would like to live, finds land there, raises the money to buy and build, presses through the months of seeking building permits, in spite of sometimes frightened and opposing neighbors, comes to agreement on the buildings and organizational structure, finds a bank willing to loan money for construction and mortgages, and finally arrives at the great day when the first residents are able to move in. Much as I wanted to live in a cohousing community, I was not a burning soul.

By January 1994, I was a member of three groups—the one with Carla; NorShorCoHo; and a group of twelve households calling themselves NWIS (the Northwest Inner Suburban Cohousing Group). The latter's flyer said the group hoped to move into its new cohousing neighborhood within two years. It would take many more years, but eventually NWIS morphed into Cornerstone Cohousing, a community that now stands about a mile from Cambridge Cohousing.

At about that time, Carla and I were working with Stella to try to get something going in Cambridge. One day, Carla called to tell me about a new cohousing group that would hold its first meeting at the Cambridge Friends Meeting House. When I got there, I looked around the brightly lit room for Carla, but I couldn't find her.

People were milling around. I felt awkward. Then I spied a couple about my age sitting at one of the long folding tables, and I took a chair next to them. Soon a tall blond woman with sharp, chiseled features clapped her hands for silence. She said she was glad we had all come and asked us to strike up a conversation with whoever was sitting near us, suggesting that we tell what brought us there and why we were interested in cohousing. Following orders, I introduced myself to the couple at my table and they told me about themselves. Joan, the woman, had a mop of curly graying hair; the man, David, was lean, with a ruddy complexion, hardly any hair, and an English accent. He said, uncomfortably, almost shame-facedly, that they were interested in cohousing because their son was. He hesitated. She, clearly annoyed with his hedging, blurted, "Our son is developmentally disabled."

A few minutes later, the tall blond woman asked us to end our conversations and move to the center of the room. By then, about twenty people had arrived. She introduced herself and her husband as Gwen and Art, architect/developers with a lot of experience in Cambridge. They were members of the Friends Meeting, which had agreed to let them use its facilities to form a cohousing community. All we had to do was clean up after ourselves.

At one point in her talk, Art interrupted, and she gave him a look that I thought I recognized as a reminder to back off. At consciousness-raising meetings over the years, I had heard many women talk about the kind of discussions with their husbands that led to that sort of look. I had had some myself years ago as my own marriage, influenced by the women's movement, had shifted from the traditional—he brings home the bacon; she manages the house-hold and kids—to something more egalitarian. By the mid-nineties, some couples were entering marriage with assumptions of equality, but older couples had to cross a sometimes turbulent stream to get from their old roles to whatever their version of equality would be.

Gwen's look said, We've agreed, I'm leading this project. Art said, "Sorry," and backed off gracefully. I knew then that she would be top dog on this project; Art would be her helpmeet. Gwen con-tinued with her agenda, and that evening we formed two commit-tees: one to draft a vision statement and another to act as a steering committee to organize future meetings. Membership on both committees was voluntary. I was still living in New Haven; I didn't join either committee.

In a sense, I was being the bane of all attempts to build a commons or a community—a freeloader, someone who benefits from the work of others but does not contribute.

TWO

Cambridge Cohousing
Is Born

1995

Sometimes cohousing is compared or confused with other types of what are generally called "intentional communities," with the communes of the sixties, or with religious settlements such as those of the Amish, or with nineteenth-century utopian experimental communities such as Brook Farm. But, unlike the many intentional communities that begin with a strong leader or a guiding moral code, cohousing communities are leaderless and they have no generally established spiritual or ideological base beyond the secular belief that it would be better to live in a communal setting and it would be good to follow green living practices. In the absence of leaders and guiding belief systems, almost all cohousing communities begin by developing a vision statement.

A communication signed "Urban Cohousing Group Statement of Purpose, approved June 27, 1991" had been circulating through many of the groups I had joined while I was looking for a cohousing community. I didn't pay much attention to it because I thought such exercises were a waste of time, producing a bunch of lofty words puffed up by dreamers. I recognized many of its phrases in the vision statement that Gwen presented at our second meeting.

As a plan to get us started, it seemed okay. It said we wanted to build in Cambridge . . . check. It said we wanted diversity . . . check. It said we would be within walking distance of public transportation and would emphasize other environmentally sound practices . . . check. It said we would have common gardens, children's play areas, general recreation space, and private gardens. Nothing wrong with that, I thought at the time. It said we would follow a consensus-based process of decision making respectful of all points of view . . . check. What was there not to like about it? Everybody at that second meeting agreed to it.

From there, we set out to structure our organization. We agreed that everyone would attend our "core" meetings, which would be held monthly at the Friends Meeting House, and there would be committees and subcommittees that would meet at Gwen and Art's office, or at the facilitators' homes. We formed the diversity committee; the membership and outreach committee, led by Stella (the same Stella who was heading up CCGB and was now working for Gwen and Art); and the finance and affordability committee, headed by Art.

By June, we were publishing a regular newsletter. Just under the logo were a few lines in italics recounting our brief history: "In February 1995, a group of people interested in forming a cohousing community in Cambridge, Mass gathered in the Cambridge Friends Meeting House. They have continued to meet there monthly as a larger group, and more often in specific interest groups at various other locations."

At a core meeting on June 21, Stella said that we needed a more formal organization, with membership rules. She proposed guidelines, and by consensus we formed a two-tier structure: Full membership would entail a nonrefundable fee of $250, joining one committee, attending the core meetings or doing some alternate service, and attending a consensus workshop. Associate members would have most of the same rights and responsibilities, but they would pay a lower nonrefundable fee of one hundred dollars, they could not block consensus, and they would have to become full members within three months of joining the group. Members in both categories would make up the core group, which would "make decisions, respond to opportunities, provide identity and community, get work done, and provide seed money." I chose to be a full member.

With that agreement, we set two very different systems of social organization in motion. One was ordinary real estate development and had to do with markets. It was reciprocal, a balance struck between sides, as in any commercial contract. Ordinarily, when a home is bought, the purchaser and seller agree on a price and a few other details and the deal is done—no need for the parties to ever see each other again. But starting out as we were with a list of agreements and obligations, we were building not only our homes but also our community, our commons; and that involved pooling. At Cambridge Cohousing, the buyers and the builders would live together possibly for the rest of their lives, sharing the common facilities and the social organization of the community, including a complicated web of relationships and friendships.

When he explained the differences between "reciprocity" and "pooling," the anthropologist Marshall Sahlins was also explaining some of the differences between a market, which calls for reciprocity, and a common, which calls for pooling. Pooling, he said, involves "collection from members of a group, often under one hand, and redivision within this group." It is the action of commoners forming a commons. Reciprocity, on the other hand, emphasizes relations where there are sides, such as in a market with buyers on one side and sellers on the other. Pooling is the collective action of a group. "Thus," said Sahlins, "pooling is the complement of social unity . . . whereas, reciprocity is the complement of social duality and 'symmetry.' Pooling stipulates a social center . . . and a social boundary . . . within which persons (or subgroups) are cooperatively related." (Sahlins, 188-9) Reciprocity is what people do in markets. Pooling, on the other hand, is what people do in commons. Like all people, we were experienced in both reciprocal and pooling relationships when we agreed to the arrangement Stella presented, and we did not go into much analysis and thought about it. But as I have been telling our story, I've found these terms and the contrast between markets and commons a big help in understanding what we were doing.

Pooling and commons are useful concepts not only to distinguish a cohousing condominium from ordinary condominiums but also to understand why we were going to a whole lot of trouble just to assuage our isolation and loneliness. Commons encourage communal behavior and that, in turn, encourages us to act in ways that are likely to make us less lonely. The more we would do together, the less lonely we would feel. It follows that in the division of space between our private units and our commons, the more space shared by our commons, the more communal or friendly our community would be.

• • •

With money coming in, we would need a bank account and a treasurer. Viv, a plump school nurse whom I had met when I joined NorShorCoHo and who would be giving up a house on the beautiful marshes north of Boston to join us, became our treasurer and opened a bank account in our name. At the June 29 meeting, she reported a balance of $2,375—the fees of ten full and ten associate members, less expenses. At that meeting, Florence, a lawyer who had grown up in England and retained more than a slight accent, reported on the organization committee. They suggested that we create a steering committee made up of two members from each of the three main committees, which by that time had become finance, membership, and site selection. All meetings were open to all members.

I attended the next steering committee meeting at Gwen and Art's condo. As it was breaking up and people were chatting and putting on their jackets, I noticed Florence and Gwen looking at me and nodding. I was being appraised. Gwen approached and asked if I would facilitate the next core group meeting. I was pleased to be noticed and judged competent; I happily agreed. The July 1995 newsletter announced the meeting, which would be held on Monday, July 10, at 7:00 P.M. in the Friends Room of the Cambridge Friends Meeting House. On the agenda were updates from the committees and plans for a Cape Cod retreat. It concluded: "Diane Margolis has generously agreed to be the facilitator for that meeting."

That meeting was a disaster. It was the first of several occasions when I wished that I had paid more attention to our vision statement. Words I hardly noticed and would not have appreciated even if I had noticed them—"We intend to follow a consensus-based process"—came back to bite me. More than a decade later, in 2011, consensus would become the decision-making method of the Occupy movement and many other grassroots organizations looking for something cozier, more participatory, more egalitarian, and less competitive than representational democracy. But in the mid-1990s, it was not often the process by which groups made decisions. More commonly, small meetings followed *Robert's Rules of Order,* a manual for parliamentary procedures, written by Brig. Gen. Henry Martyn Robert, first published in 1876, and followed by almost all the groups I had belonged to, from the town meetings of Wilton, Connecticut, to the meetings of the American Sociological Association. I knew it pretty well.

Consensus, on the other hand, was not much practiced in the late twentieth century except by Quakers and radical social justice groups such as SNCC, Food Not Bombs, and anarchists. For them, the appeal of consensus was that, rather than giving power to majorities and weakening minorities, consensus protects the voice of the least member, even if it is a minority of one. Like markets, parliamentary procedures concentrate power at the top by weakening those at the bottom, while, like commons, consensus empowers minorities. Its goal is to reach decisions using methods that equitably involve all parties to the agreement.

My only experience with consensus had been with the League of Women Voters. The League used it to decide the goals it would pursue each year. I once asked the leader of our Wilton group why we used such a cumbersome method, and she explained that, as a volunteer organization, it was important that everybody had an opportunity to participate in deciding what we would work on each year, so that, when a plan was chosen, everybody would participate. With a vote, especially a close vote, almost half the group might be against the position taken and it would be difficult to get the energy and participation needed to act. That was all I knew and all I thought I needed to know about consensus when I arrived at the Friends Meeting House on July 10, 1995, at about 6:45 P.M.

Some people were already there. I began helping to arrange the tables and chairs into a large circle so we could all see one another. There was no head to the table, nor was there a place to put a newsprint pad, where we might have been able to display the agenda. As I sat down, Gwen took the seat to my left and mumbled something about wanting to talk about past troubles. I couldn't make out exactly what she was saying. I asked if she wanted to start off with that. She said no. I asked when she would like to speak. She said she didn't know. I said it was getting late and that I would have to call the meeting to order.

And so the meeting began. As we had at previous meetings, I started with a reading of the agenda and said that reports of committees would follow announcements. Viv, who was sitting a few seats to my right, gave the treasurer's report, affirming that she had opened a bank account and stating its balance. As she concluded, she said she had a question for the group to decide: Would we pay for babysitters at the retreat we were planning at Gwen and Art's place on the Cape? Before Viv or I could take another breath, a woman sitting to Viv's right said that she had raised her children and paid for her own babysitting and she was not about to pay for anybody else's. Gwen quickly responded that we wanted parents to participate and therefore we should pay for babysitting.

With that, we were off and running: Everyone had an opinion and everyone stated it without waiting to be called. I broke into the din and said I'd make a list and call on everybody who wanted to speak (a process that I later learned is called "stacking"). That worked for a little while, but soon everyone was again talking at once. Fearing that things had gotten out of hand, I asked if someone would make a proposal on which we could vote.

"We don't vote," a bunch of people said in unison. "We use consensus."

"Okay," I said, "then we need to come to consensus on whether we will pay for babysitting at the retreat. Wouldn't it be good to have a proposal?"

Again, everyone spoke at once. Then above the babble someone said that we should stop and wait for the light.

If my suggestion that we vote had put me on shaky ground, the suggestion that we wait for the light sent me whirling down a rabbit hole. The thought streaked through my mind that waiting for the light might be something like opening the door at a seder so the prophet Elijah could step in for a sip of wine. I asked how we would know when the light had come. A few people, probably all of them Quakers, groaned.

Another thought streaked through my mind: Maybe this cohousing community is only for Quakers and I don't belong here.

I suggested that we put the babysitter question aside until the end of the meeting and treat it as new business. That brought quiet and order. We went on to the next committee report: planning for the retreat.

When all the committee reports were completed and we were about to turn to new business, I asked Gwen again if this would be a good time for her to say what she had to say. She said no. I asked when. Again, she said she didn't know. I never did find out what she wanted to say, but at the retreat I told her that her request and indecision had made it difficult for me to facilitate the meeting. She apologized for being "brain-dead."

Finding a Compromise Between the Common Good and the Individual

When we returned to the question of babysitting at the retreat, we somehow reached consensus on a compromise between the two highly principled positions that were at stake: the individualistic position that those who had passed their babysitter-paying days should not subsidize other people's babysitters and the equally highly principled communal position that if the community wanted the participation of parents, it would have to pay for babysitters. The consensus was that at formal meetings there would be a babysitter paid for by the community, but there wouldn't be one throughout the weekend.

That was the first of dozens of decisions large and small that would shape our community. Most of them were moments when our community would have to choose between the two central philosophies that guide most contemporary democracies. On the one hand, there is the common good; on the other, there is private property. On the one hand, we were building a community that many of us hoped would lead us to a less lonely existence; on the other hand, we were building our homes, for most of us our largest investment in private property. On the one hand, we were resting on the philosophies of the Left that had brought us the democracies of Western civilization; on the other, we were drawing support from philosophies of the Right that were bringing us market triumphalism and the second enclosure, that set of new, grossly expanded copyright laws that Duke Law School professor James Boyle says are now enclosing "the intangible commons of the mind" (Boyle 2003, 37). Often, as in this case, we would find a way for both sides to have their cake and eat some of it.

In spite of the happy solution we found to the babysitting question, I went home feeling bruised and wondering whether I would survive consensus. Off and on since then, I've wondered what it meant to "wait for the light" and, finally, I looked it up on the internet. Here's what a leaflet offered to newcomers at the Homewood Friends Meeting in Baltimore said:

> Our worship is based on silence. . . . Quaker worship is an alert openness to the still leading of the Inner Light. One consequence of this "waiting upon the Light" is that one or more worshipers may be moved to speak out of the silence. Such speaking . . . is a movement from the depths of one's being, a conscientious response to a carefully discerned leading of the Spirit. . . . (Homewood Friends 2015)

How any of the Quakers at our meeting thought that an Inner Light might shine through the pandemonium of everyone talking at once is a mystery. The apprehension that I had inadvertently joined an exclusively Quaker group must have been shared by others, for Gwen began the next core meeting by saying that some people had asked her whether this cohousing group was going to be only for Quakers and she wanted to assure us that it was not.

That was a relief. Not that I had anything against Quakers. In those days, I thought Quakers had a lot going for them. The few I knew had an appealing settled and sensible air about them, and

I admired their nonviolence and the work of the American Friends Service Committee. Twice I had applied for admission to Quaker institutions—once to a Friends summer camp and once to Swarthmore College. Both times I had been rejected. I didn't hold that against the Friends, figuring that I just wasn't good enough. I would have liked to measure up and felt that if I were ever to put an end to my agnostic nonchalance, I might check out the Quakers—along with the Unitarian Universalists and Reform Jewish congregations.

We Learn a Bit About Consensus

A highlight of the retreat at Gwen and Art's house was a consensus workshop. I was especially struck when the presenters said the facilitator needed to prepare in advance by calling all those who wanted to be on the agenda to find out what they wanted to present and to make sure that it would be presented in the best way. Had I done that, I might have decided with Viv that it would be best to introduce the babysitter question after the committee reports had been completed. Then we could have introduced it as a proposal. Perhaps we might have made it part of our planning for the retreat, but certainly it would not have popped up unexpectedly at the tail end of her treasurer's report.

The presenters also introduced the idea of colored cards, something that we, like many cohousing communities, used. At the beginning of our general meetings, we each got a set of three cards (red, green, and yellow), which we raised during discussions to signal to the facilitator that we wished to make a comment (green), offer clarification (yellow), or stop the process because we thought something was going very wrong (red). When there was a call for consensus on a proposal, we raised a green card to approve, a yellow card to approve with reservations, or a red card to reject. Just one red card would send the proposal back to its presenters for revisions.

After the retreat, at the next general meeting, Gwen distributed a draft from the organization committee of suggested guidelines for cohousing meetings. There is no manual that does for consensus what *Robert's Rules* does for parliamentary groups. Communities that want to use consensus decision making need to develop their own guidelines, aided by one or another of the few guidebooks that address consensus. We decided to use a handbook by Lawrence Butler and Amy Rothstein entitled *On Conflict and Consensus,* which purports to give guidelines. It became our *Robert's Rules,* but it is not nearly as detailed and precise as *Robert's Rules* and it often left us groping through dark corridors, where the loudest voices took the lead.

For about a decade, we limped along with consensus, until we followed many other cohousing communities and shifted to a more formal form of consensus sometimes called "sociocracy" and sometimes called "dynamic governance." The chief weaknesses of consensus were that it gave inordinate power to anyone willing to raise a red card and to the loudest voices. In return for those weaknesses came its many benefits over voting. For a commons, a group that wants to be a community of equals, voting has many drawbacks: It creates winners and losers; it generates factions and division; rather than searching for the solution to a problem that is satisfactory to all and abhorrent to none, it forces decisions into just two possible solutions and thus can prevent compromise; where the vote is close, almost half the community members become losers and are likely to drag their heels when it comes to implementation; where the vote is private, it introduces secrecy into a community where a major strength is common knowledge; and, finally, it is competitive rather than cooperative. Consensus is thus a better system for a commons, a community of equals. It allows all voices to be heard as the group searches for solutions to problems that are acceptable to all.

Diversity and Its Discontents

Through the fall of 1995, we focused on three projects: developing an organizational structure, finding land, and building membership. We wanted diversity, all kinds of diversity: people of color; people at various stages in their life cycle, especially families with young children; and people at various income levels, including some members who could afford to help make the payments necessary to buy land and begin building. Cohousers across the country share a yearning for diversity among members, especially racial and economic diversity. To achieve it at Cambridge Cohousing, we created the affordability committee at our second meeting. It began exploring ways to have units that would be affordable for people who could not pay the full price of a unit. We began by looking into government and charitable subsidies, but it wasn't looking good. Art laid out our choices: If we wanted to have deep subsidies on some of our units, we would have to hire a consultant, and that would cost anywhere from five thousand dollars to twenty thousand. To justify that expenditure, we would need six to eight members who could qualify for a deep subsidy from the federal government. We had about that number who had asked to be exempt from the membership fees, but only one of them could qualify for a Section 8 voucher, the usual form of housing assistance from the federal government. Among the others, only one was in the government's low-income category. Art also thought that government regulations would require the subsidized units to be under separate ownership, probably grouped apart from the rest of the community—in short, ghettoized. That wasn't what those who asked for exemptions or any of the rest of us had in mind. Moreover, because we didn't already have them, we would have to recruit people who could qualify for those units.

By October, the contrary goals of diversity and some members well-heeled enough to pay for the land when we found it were becoming apparent, and the membership committee distributed a paper stating the difficulties:

> There are questions we have been pondering in order to reconcile our need for financial viability and our wish to comply with our Vision Statement's intent to establish diversity in our membership. At this point in our development, we need people who will not need any financial exemptions, therefore we have prioritized our membership needs as follows: people who can afford to pay the full price for their units; families with children; people of color; people in their 20s or early 30s. . . . We welcome your thoughts on this matter!

Meanwhile, the Site Search committee was looking at sites that Gwen had discovered. The search for a building site in Cambridge had stymied all the other nascent groups I had joined. Cambridge lies across the Charles River from Boston. Its largest employer is Harvard University, the second largest is MIT (Massachusetts Institute of Technology). Those institutions owned large portions of Cambridge and made any real estate they did not own attractive. The end of rent control in 1994 escalated the value of residential real estate. There was hardly any vacant land in Cambridge, and whatever there was, was expensive.

Discovering building sites where no one else could was Gwen's specialty. She knew Cambridge. She knew where all the possible building sites were. From day one, she had sites to show us. By the fall of 1995, she had identified seven sites that met most of the four criteria that we had agreed were important to us: quiet, safety, clean air, and walking distance to the T. Under her guidance, a small ad hoc site search committee, which I joined when I could, set out to visit several of them. Gwen was impressive. In no time at all, as we walked from site to site, she made sketches to show how we could place our buildings on each new piece of land.

In our November newsletter, Gwen said she was contacting the two most favored sites' owners to ascertain that in fact they were both ready and willing to discuss a possible purchase. "Obviously," she wrote, "the biggest question is $." It would take a lot of background work to ascertain if there could be a "meeting of interests and resources" for a site purchase. "Things COULD get exciting again quite soon. More to report on the 25th, hopefully with pictures!"

Standard wisdom in cohousing circles is that once a group has found its site, it is up and running. Many cohousing communities fall apart because they fail to agree on a site. The Winter 1992 issue of the *Northeast Coho/US Northern Quarterly,* a publication of the National Cohousing Organization, listed four groups in Connecticut. None of them got off the ground, or, to be more precise, none of them got to the point where they could buy the ground on which to build. A particularly sad and angry story was printed several years later on Cohousing-L, the national Listserv started in 1993 by cohouser Fred Olsen.

> Hello from West Hartford, CT—Two years ago (though it feels like 10) when I hung up my first cohousing flyer in this state, I wanted to pick my favorite town and call it Canton Cohousing and see who showed up for the first meeting.
>
> I was advised by a cohousing consultant not to do that, but instead to cast as wide a net as possible. Reluctantly, I called it Greater Hartford Cohousing and scattered my flyers around various towns. In retrospect, I should have stuck to my original plan.
>
> Here is why: We now have ten financially committed households. There are 29 towns circling Hartford. Our group is from all over the state. We have collectively pooled almost 30K in our bank account and have paid cohousing consultants 10K for help with site selection, pro forma, and guidance. Their contract has ended.

Connecticut Magazine is reserving space for a cover story when we choose our site . . . but we just can't do it. Several sites have come up and we could actively have pursued three sites, but it always ends up that maybe 5 or 6 households want to and the others don't.

To complicate matters, only 2 households of the 10 have small children (me being one of them). We want more families. A new site has hit the horizon now and the majority of the singles like it and are getting angry that the two families don't. The high school has a 33% drop out rate and is perceived as a weaker school system.

If we land in a school that is perceived as lousy, I can forget my dream of lots of children running around. The singles think we are too picky and are saying if we want more diversity, we have to move to a lower socioeconomic town with less attractive schools.

The two families want a higher economic town with good schools and welcome diversity there. (Surprise!)

I am tired. Our meetings are starting to be irritating. Our consultants are gone and we need help.

If anyone has ideas on how a group of ten households with totally different viewpoints, etc. can come together on one site . . . please let us know. Our meeting is Monday and I would like to share any responses we get. Newbies, pick your favorite town and go for it.

Thanks everyone.

8 Jun 2001
Shelly DeMeo
Greater Hartford Cohousing

First in Connecticut, media watching and waiting . . . and waiting . . . and waiting . . .

If Shelly DeMeo continued to wait and work for a cohousing community in Connecticut, she would still be waiting. By 2021, there weren't any cohousing communities in Connecticut, though one group was trying to form—as had many over the years.

Meanwhile, there were more than a dozen communities in Massachusetts. Probably the reason Massachusetts has offered more fertile ground for cohousing than Connecticut is that Connecticut has greater income inequality, with a higher percentage of residents living in areas of concentrated wealth or poverty. Shelly DeMeo's impossible challenge to find a town in Connecticut for her cohousing community and our need to prioritize members who could make a full down payment have similar roots.

Like it or not—and most of us did not like it when our membership committee announced its revised list of priorities, headed by the ability to pay—cohousing is not built on a level or pristine field. It is nested in a world with limited choices and we had come up against a major contradiction between the diversity goals we espoused for our community and our individual goals for career advancement and increasing wealth. We wanted to live in Cambridge, a mostly white, middle-class community. Like Shelly DeMeo, we wanted to live in a town with good schools and would welcome diversity there.

The cost of land and therefore housing had put us beyond the budgets of those who might bring us economic and racial diversity. Cohousing is a home ownership model, a condition that makes diversity difficult because the pool of minority members is slim. In the Boston area in 2019, the average net worth of African Americans was close to zero, the average net worth of whites was $247,500 (Munoz et al. 2015). That disparity was built on different opportunities to grow equity; a long history going back to our country's beginnings in slavery, followed by centuries of discriminatory practices such as redlining and predatory mortgage lending. Most of us, as members of the privileged majority, not the discriminated-against minority, would be selling the homes we lived in to release the down payment we needed to buy into our cohousing community. Most Blacks had not yet bought their first home and had not begun the long process of building equity in a home. Shelly DeMeo was not willing to send her kids to a school with a 33 percent dropout rate. No parent would choose such a school for their children, which is why most cohousing communities across the country are in white, middle-class towns.

That made Cambridge Cohousing look a bit like a gated community, a charge leveled against the cohousing movement but refuted by most researchers (Ruiu 2014; Chiodelli 2015; Boyer and Leland 2018), architects, and geographers. The similarities underlying that charge are that both cohousing communities and gated communities are home ownership models with shared facilities. The differences are that gated communities are built with high walls and other devices to keep outsiders out, while most cohousing communities are built to create community and most welcome their neighbors. The problem for cohousing communities is that they must buy into established housing markets that exclude those they would like to include. Gradually, with great effort and some luck, cohousing nationwide has become somewhat more diverse, and by 2019, Cambridge Cohousing did include several people of color. But that would be many years off.

Given that the average cost of land for each unit would be about $35,000 and we would have to pay for construction at market rates, it didn't look as though we could build affordable units without a subsidy. What we wanted was a government or private organization to help us build affordable units for those who were already members of our group. We wanted their units to be indistinguishable from the rest of the units, and we didn't want to have to go looking for new members who could qualify.

Carla, the woman with whom I had tried to form a group to build in Cambridge, wanted us to set aside some units for diversity, as she said Pioneer Valley, a cohousing community in Western Massachusetts, had done. She didn't feel we were strongly enough committed to our diversity goals and wanted us to have a retreat to review our community's identity and think about what membership meant to us. Gwen said that would be unnecessary, as our vision statement answered those questions. Florence wondered if we should struggle to have affordability, but Gwen wasn't quite ready to give up on it and said that we were lucky to be in Cambridge, which "has many citizens committed to high-quality affordable housing" and that she had faith that if we kept on this track, we could get something. She added that those of us who needed a subsidy and lived in Cambridge should contact the Community Development Department, where someone named Penelope was setting up courses for first-time home buyers.

As we wavered over our diversity goals, I thought about a concept developed by the sociologist Kai Erikson. Noting the contradictory values shared by the miners he studied after a dam broke and flooded their village, leaving most of them homeless, he pointed out that cultures are not monolithic; they often emphasize opposing values, and those values tended to form along what he called "axes of variation." He wrote, "The identifying motifs of a culture are not just the core values to which people pay homage but also the lines of point and counterpoint along which they diverge. Axes of variation . . . are not only sources of tension but gradients along which responses to social change are likely to take place." (Erikson 1976, 82)

At Cambridge Cohousing, our salient axis of variation would line up along values that supported our private units at one end and values that supported our community, our commons, at the other. At one end, we would be careful to admit only members who could afford to buy a unit; at the other, we would seek economic diversity among our members. At one end, we would want consensus and assume congruent values; at the other, we would seek diversity and develop ways to explore and live with conflicting values.

On October 4, 1995, the membership committee discontinued the associate membership category. We were ready to make an offer on a site by the bike path. Some members worried that neighbors might oppose us. We needed a name, and Art, saying that we would need to approach neighbors with sensitivity, suggested that we go with plain vanilla. After trying out more than two dozen other possibilities, we settled on Cambridge Cohousing (CCH).

Over the next two months, our offer for the site by the bike path was rejected and we kept looking at other sites and adding members to our group. On December 4, still without a site, we held a lottery for the order of choosing our units. My number was 20. By that time, we had twenty-two full members: six families with children, twelve single households (nine women, three men), and four empty-nester couples. Altogether, there were twelve children under fifteen, thirteen people in their thirties and forties, twelve in their fifties and sixties, and two in their seventies. There were sixteen women and eleven men. As for diversity, there would be a special-needs household with room for four and their helper; three people of color; a mix of religious affiliations, with Quakers being the most numerous; and a range of wealth, from one member who would need a subsidy to at least four others who could afford a summer home. Carla was still trying to find a way to extend our lower range, but it was, for the most part, a lonely effort. While most members would have welcomed greater racial diversity, they were not willing to shoulder its likely costs. That funding would have to come from a government agency or a charitable foundation.

Three

Our Homes
and Our Commons

Nineteen ninety-six began with the birth of Cambridge Cohousing as a legal entity. By consensus, at the core group meeting on January 15, the steering committee was authorized to hire a lawyer to draw up the papers that would turn Cambridge Cohousing into a limited liability partnership (LLP). As an LLP, we would be able to buy land and sign contracts. Our LLP was a commons: It belonged to all of us and would be managed by all of us. Our material or physical commons would be all of our land and buildings not owned privately by any one of us. Those privately owned areas would be our units, and although we would put a lot of our thought and resources into those units, the whole point of creating CCH was the hope that we would live together in a friendly community whose members would enjoy and care about one another.

Voluntary Work and Contracts

Work lay on that axis between the market and the commons. We expect to be paid for our work in the market, but in the commons our work is freely given. As we were trying to form our community, some of us worked at it for many hours each week, but others hardly lifted a finger.

For more than a year, Art and Gwen had been working, along with the rest of us, as volunteers. However, when a commons requires special experience or skills and when it needs that work to be regularly performed, then a commons must pay for the work it needs. If we were to build a housing development, we would need a developer and our developer would expect to be paid.

On May 20, after we had been meeting and looking for land for more than a year and had finally made an offer that we expected would be accepted, we met to sign a contract with Gwen and Art to be our developers. David, the man I met at the first meeting, presented a draft of the formal agreement. Art explained the agreement, pointing out that both he and Gwen were architects as well as developers. They would do the schematic design but would hire an architect to complete the design development. "We won't be sitting at the drawing board," said Gwen, "and we're already building the team." They assured us that they knew all about architects' egos and runaway budgets and we could count on them to keep moving ahead without budget increases. Gwen also said that she would superintend construction so we would not have to hire and pay for a project manager.

When someone complained that all the cohousing developments he had seen in Massachusetts were boxy, Art and Gwen assured us that our design would be great and that their plan to use a modular company would save a large portion of the architectural cost. There were some more questions and then Art and Gwen left the room so we could discuss the contract.

There were questions and answers about the schedule of payments to Art and Gwen. Someone pointed out that 7 percent of seven million dollars, the projected cost of our development, was a lot of money and we needed to fight for every bit of savings so that we could have diversity, but David pointed out that there was a $320,000 maximum for the contract even if the cost of the project rose. "Art doesn't want more for the same work," he said, noting that Gwen and Art had worked for free so far, and they had kept the group together all this time. There was a discussion, which included warnings about timing, one person pointing out that construction usually tends to drag, increasing the expense of a project, but that was countered by someone who said that if construction dragged on, it would probably be largely our own fault. David pointed out that Art and Gwen were part of the community and were working hard already. To which someone noted that members might not be the best workers. Carla then said that they had a strong incentive for enhancing their professional reputation. Frank a short, pixyish man who often touted a wisdom he claimed to have gained from membership in other cohousing communities, said it was important to communicate really well, especially where there were conflicts. He pointed out that New View had looked for land for four years and considered sixty sites, and we had found our site in one year, which was phenomenal. "If we move in next spring, we deserve a prize," he said.

We called Art and Gwen back into the room. We told them that those present accepted the agreement. Gwen said that the purchase and sale agreement for the land on Richdale Avenue was on her desk and that she had gotten the owners to agree to include the demolition of existing structures in the price of $1,340,000. They then promised that if we followed their suggestion and used Green Village ecodynamic boxes, we could move in by the following spring. The plan was to start construction in December. With new materials, Gwen said, we could pour concrete in freezing weather and get much more favorable pricing from ecodynamic builders because they had less work in the winter. We could plan to move into the town houses first and have the rest of the community in by July 1997. She added that now that we had our site, efficiency would become very important; we needed to make decisions in the most expeditious way possible, using the developers' skills to the fullest.

Looking back on that day, I often wonder why we were all such lambs. What was I thinking? Clearly not much. I just sat there, going along with everything, asking no questions, doing no checking, just plunking down my dollars and my signature. My son is a lawyer; I didn't even ask him to read over the contract. Ed and Barbara said that they were asking their lawyer to go over the contract, and I thought, Why should I go to the trouble and the expense of getting my lawyer to go over the same territory? Probably our biggest mistake was to accept Gwen's offer to act as project manager at no additional cost, but other stipulations, such as a penalty for delay and some restriction on the hiring of subcontractors, might have helped.

Once again, I was being a freeloader. But I considered the price of raising questions. Carla kept trying. She was particularly interested in affordability and wanted us to review the values that had brought us together. But each time she asked for a retreat to review our values, Gwen quashed the idea, preventing discussion by saying that we had all we needed in our vision statement. No one, not I, nor apparently anyone else, wanted to hear more from Carla about values; no one wanted to buck Gwen, at least not for anything as nebulous as values. Some people even made fun of Carla.

Once, not long after we signed the contract with Gwen and Art, while Carla was talking, I noticed Deb smirking and looking around the room for confirmation. I felt awful but said nothing. How do you complain about a smirk? And if you do, what's the chance that you will be the butt of the next smirk? Bullying can be subtle; it can be scary. It's a way to exert power outside the rules of a commons and what we often consider common decency. The coronavirus pandemic provides an example of the choice a community has when, for instance, someone does not have the common decency to wear a mask. Some states will use mandates to force individuals to wear masks for the sake of the common good; others will invoke ideas of liberty as death rates rise—two end points on an axis of variation.

One of the greatest misunderstandings about commons is that they work without government or management. As David Bollier says, "a commons is a resource + a community + a set of social protocols." (Bollier 2014, 15) Just because you can use something without paying for it does not mean that you can use it freely, no rules attached. There will be rule breakers in every commons; there will be people like Deb who can be mean and disruptive at times. Every community must find a way to govern its members.

The myth that commons do not need to be governed was perpetuated by Garrett Hardin, who wrote an article so influential that it probably set back our understanding of commons by decades. This article, "The Tragedy of the Commons," argued that commons were doomed because everybody would misuse them (Hardin, 1968). His example was a field for grazing. He argued that individuals would add to their flocks until the land was depleted. He was possibly right. Given the chance, many of us would abuse the commons, until it was destroyed. His solution was to turn all commons into private property, arguing that an owner would take care of his land and not pasture more animals than the land could support. What Hardin failed to recognize was that all commons need to be managed, and all commoners need to be governed. Usually, we do not recognize that commons are being governed, because many natural commons are so plentiful that it takes a long time to notice that they are being depleted. Or, what is perhaps more usual, care for the commons is so ingrained in a culture that its principles seem a part of nature.

In those early days, we did not take the time to review our goals as Carla wanted us to do, but we did not join Deb in making fun of Carla, either. Would it have made a difference? I doubt it.

Most of those who had until then taken leadership positions were in favor of signing the contract with Art and Gwen. All I wanted, maybe all anybody wanted, was to move into our new community as soon as possible. Signing that contract seemed to be the best way to do it.

Maybe I was a lamb, but I did not, and do not, think I was being led to slaughter. It's 2021 as I write this and I am living in Cambridge Cohousing. I am happy to be here. I can't think of anyplace else I'd rather be living. More than two-thirds of the people who joined the LLP that signed the contract with Gwen and Art are my fellow cohousers, still here after more than two decades.

Of course, there is much about the life of our community that I would change if I could. Looking back, I see moments when our actions, while getting us the homes we wanted, were simultaneously preventing us from getting the community we said we wanted. We probably didn't all have the same idea of the community we wanted. But how would we have known? Once we agreed to our vision statement at our second meeting, we spent little time discussing the life of our community. Our focus was on construction.

In those early days, as we signed contracts and checks with gay abandon, we were gay—in the old sense: cheerful and optimistic. As Frank pointed out on the day we signed our contract with Gwen and Art, it takes most cohousing communities many years to come as far as we had in little more than a year. If cohousing communities were running races to see which could get from initial meeting to move-in the fastest, Cambridge Cohousing would probably win the prize. Like the many groups that I belonged to before I joined Cambridge Cohousing, most cohousing groups fail before they are able to find and purchase a piece of land. Only we and Cornerstone, of all those groups, came to fruition. Cornerstone had formed two years before we did and they finally moved into their site a mile away from Cambridge Cohousing five years after we moved into ours.

Four

Blind Visionaries

Summer 1996

When June came, I graded my final exams and papers and booked a room in Rockport, Massachusetts, for the summer. Someone once asked a colleague why he'd left a high-paying position in the business world to teach at a university. He quickly responded, as every professor and teacher might, "Three reasons: June, July, and August." I decided to spend my June, July, and August in Rockport for three additional reasons: One, my son Philip, his wife, and their two daughters were living there; two, Rockport is a beautiful seaside town that hosts a major summer music festival; and, three, it is less than an hour from Cambridge, where we were galumphing forward and meeting three or four times a week. We had our land, Gwen and Art had their contract, many of us had made our down payment, and we had left in the dust all those other groups trying to form a cohousing community in Cambridge.

As far as I could tell, we were all in high spirits. At the June 10 core group meeting, Gwen had announced that the purchase and sale agreement was in the sellers' hands and she expected their signatures soon. Six of us had put up the capital to buy the land. Practicing consensus by using our colored cards, we raised green ones, giving Viv, David, and Florence the power to sign our documents. We set up a development oversight committee (DOC) made up of David, Florence, Barbara, Carla, and Sheila. They would meet at Gwen and Art's office every Tuesday from 5:00 to 6:30 and whenever else a quick decision was needed. The DOC would link the community and the developers. No one questioned this decision at the core meeting. As was our usual practice those days, the organization committee made its proposal and gave its reasons—"We now need a small committee that is able to meet several times a week (often at short notice), a flexibility the large steering committee does not have"—and we all raised our green cards.

Art, who managed our finances and gave a fiscal report at every core meeting, announced that we had $110,000 on deposit, $50,000 of which would be paid as a deposit when the P&S came back. He warned that everyone should be ready to make their 30 percent down payment so that we would have the money we needed to buy the land and start building. That wasn't easy for those members who were buying their first home or had their equity tied up in their old homes. So, in hopes of increasing our economic diversity, we said some people would be exempt from making the full down payment until we were ready to move in and they could get mortgages. They became "the exempts." Most of us didn't know who they were.

We wanted to be a multigenerational community, and at core meetings of the community, Joan, the facilitator of the membership committee, let us know how close we were coming to our goal of filling all our units and having one-third of our units housing for singles, one-third for families with children under fifteen, and one-third for households with two or more adults. By June, we had twenty-one households. Four more were on the waiting list, but they were all singles, and we already had our full quota of singles; we needed more families with young children.

At our June 10 meeting, Don and I presented a proposal for changes we hoped would help us attract young families. Our first suggestion was to change our core meeting time to Sunday. Then we proposed, and the group quickly reached consensus, to have child care at all core meetings—we had come a long way from the day when the suggestion to provide child care could shatter a meeting. We also suggested that the organization committee change its name to the social organization and community life committee and have two functions: to suggest rules for the community and responsibilities for its members, and to organize opportunities to get together socially with one another. The committee needed new members, especially people who were interested in organizing social activities. Ellen, who had just become a member, dubbed herself the "frivolity facilitator," and began coming to meetings wearing a jester's hat.

Stella had said early on that developing a cohousing community was different from a standard development. But I doubt that anyone realized how very different our process would be, especially not Gwen and Art, who knew a lot about real estate development but were as new as the rest of us to cohousing.

If we had been building our own single-family homes, we would have hired an architect and, with her or him, planned the building. But we were over twenty households planning our homes together. That usually requires a developer. Ordinarily, the developer's job is to set the ball rolling by bringing in, when necessary, the people to fill all the roles that a real estate development needs: investors, architects, builders, appraisers, interior decorators, and landscapers, to list but a few of the specialists who help build large projects. In multiunit residential developments like ours, unit owners usually don't come onstage until the project is almost complete. Cohousing, by contrast, begins with the future residents; they are the investors.

Freed by our LLP from some parts of the development process, Gwen could focus on her most creative talents—finding a site in land-scarce Cambridge, imagining our buildings' footprint on our long, narrow strip of land between the commuter rail tracks and Richdale Avenue, knowing how to have her plans accepted by neighbors and town boards, and bringing in and coordinating all the specialists. The less creative, riskier parts of the development process would be handled by the rest of us. Our LLP would put up the money for the land, the LLP would get a building loan for the construction, and there would be no nail-biting delay or danger of bankruptcy for the developers if the real estate market were to turn down and buyers for all the units could not be found.

The other side of the coin for Gwen was that, whereas in an ordinary condo development the future owners would not even have been on the scene during the building process, we cohousers were there from day one and we thought we were doing something very special that required different procedures. For example, in an ordinary development, the developer would decide which common facilities the community would have, while in a cohousing community, the cohousers decide and they may choose those facilities for very different reasons than a developer of a commercial housing development would.

Many condominiums have common facilities, and some of them are far more extensive than anything a cohousing community could afford. At the high end, some commercial condominiums and gated communities feature health clubs with indoor and outdoor pools, exercise rooms, tennis courts, and even golf courses. No cohousing community has all those amenities, because almost all of them, unlike high-end condo communities, want to be inclusive, not exclusive. The whole point of common facilities in a cohousing community is not to get the biggest bang for your buck when you put the units on the market, but to bring cohousers together into a shared life so that everyone could be inoculated against what the surgeon general had called the "epidemic of loneliness."

Some writers on the commons have used the word *commoning* to denote the collective action of a group. Lewis Hyde, for example, says, "I want 'common' to be available as a verb (as in this from an old book on British law: 'Generally a man may common in a forest')." (Hyde 2010, 27) Because we were commoning, we had to plan our common house together. Barbara, the facilitator of the design committee, was in charge of bringing us all together on a plan for our common facilities. At a core meeting, she handed each of us a sheet with two columns; one was headed "Basics," the other "Would Likes." On the "Basics" list was the entrance to the common house, the living room, the dining room, the kitchen, a kids' area, a tot lot, passageways, and lawns. The "Would Likes" list included such things as a fireplace, a soundproof music room, a library, a hot tub, a TV room, and a pool. Barbara said we could add items or switch them from the "Basics" list to the "Would Likes" list, or vice versa.

As we discussed each item, we made many decisions. We decided to locate the entrance and the mail room so that everyone would have to pass through them on their way to their units, thus increasing the chances that we'd all see one another frequently. The living room, we decided, should not be a passageway, but an area with spaces for different moods. The dining room should have a deck or patio at the same level so we could eat outside in the summer, and it should be able to double as a meeting room. Then we decided that most of the common rooms should be designed so they could have more than one purpose. The kitchen would be near the kids' space so that cooks could watch their kids while they helped to prepare meals. There would be a tot lot that would be very safe, but then Becky pointed out that we should integrate kids throughout the community and make the whole place safe for kids. There would be covered and uncovered passageways between units. Gwen would call the major passageway that would run from the eastern to the western boundary of our long narrow lot "the spine," and to maximize interaction among residents, we decided that it would have special attractions that would draw people to either end. We would also have an open lawn, and Gwen said that if we planned the space well, we could have plenty of room for orchards and gardens.

I imagined myself a year or so in the future strolling through shaded pathways that opened onto brilliant sunny glades, where I could stop for a chat or read by a bubbling fountain. It all seemed idyllic and possible, especially as we moved on to Barbara's "Would Like" list. At that point, each household was given a little packet with twelve sticky dots: three blue ones (worth four points each), three red ones (worth three points each), three yellow ones (worth two points each), and three green ones (worth one point each). One by one, we went to the master list in the front of the room and put our dots alongside the facilities we wanted. When everyone was finished, we counted up the dots. In order of preference, our choices turned out to be a fireplace, a recreation room for older kids, a soundproof music room, a greenhouse, interior storage, a hot tub, a library, a workshop, bright sunny spots, an exercise room, a laundry, an interior water garden, a TV room, an outdoor water feature, a pool, outdoor clotheslines, and a large freezer so we could buy food in bulk. Some members pointed out that we didn't need all these amenities because nearby there was a city pool, a library, tennis and basketball courts, and a community garden. Others suggested that some facilities could be less expensive if they were built beneath the street level.

At an earlier meeting, Art had given us a general idea of what units of various sizes would cost and we had filled out forms noting the number of bedrooms we wanted. With that list and the list of common facilities, Gwen was able to come back six days later with a two-page document called "Draft Program for Site Plan & Common House." It began with a couple of paragraphs from our vision statement, reminding us that "the purpose of the Cambridge Cohousing group is to create an urban residential community in which the architectural and social organization is designed to inspire and enhance the daily lives of its inhabitants." Another paragraph from our vision statement was followed by a "description of general character of overall community." I was happy with all the amenities we had chosen at the core meeting, and Gwen's promises buoyed my spirits and confidence. Who would not be overjoyed to know they would soon be living in an environment that would "project a sense of being a spirited, contemporary community or village rooted in its New England context: simple elegance, subtle variety of forms and details but consonance of the whole"? She promised "quality construction" and "resourceful use of materials," wheelchair accessibility, and "terraces appropriate for dining al fresco," with room for "frisbee-frolicking or croquet."

Also, at that meeting, Barbara presented a survey she wanted us all to fill out. "Because our new venture has a high cost and is based on some assumptions we've had about community," said Barbara, "it would be a good idea if we were each to write our vision of community to see if we're on the same track. Remember," she said, "that community requires reciprocity, give-and-take, social agreements." She probably hadn't read Sahlins. But at that time no one was thinking in terms of the differences between commons and markets or pooling and reciprocity. Barbara said it would be a good idea if we were to reread our vision statement, which she claimed was well written and being emulated by other cohousing communities, and then write down our answers to two questions: "What do I expect to *get* from the community?" and "What do I expect to *give* to the community?" We'd do it anonymously. Barbara would collate the results for our second retreat, which we were to have in July, again at Gwen and Art's place on the Cape.

With the June 20, 1996 issue, I began editing the newsletter. I promised to try to have a newsletter in the mail within forty-eight hours of each core meeting. Each issue carried under our logo this notice: "The big push is on. From now until we submit our plans to Planning and Zoning, we'll be meeting very often. Please come to as many meetings as you can."

Most of the newsletter was devoted, as before, to the minutes Bert had taken of the previous core meeting. At the end, there was a new column titled "News from Members," which asked everyone to contribute more items. In my first issue was the news that Florence's son-in-law, Dewey Thompson, had a film, *Red Sky at Night*, featured in the Nantucket Film Festival and favorably reviewed in the *Globe;* David (the man I'd met at the CCGB meeting) and his wife, Stephanie, were moving, and David's group, The Boys of Bedlam, would be playing at the Borders in Peabody; there was a show of Mike's photography; Barbara's sister's sculpture was at the schoolhouse gallery in North Truro; and Yale University Press had accepted my second book, *Fabric of Self*, for publication.

At a meeting shortly after the DOC was formed, Florence gave its report, laying out plans for designing our buildings and choosing a builder. She promised unit meetings in the next couple of weeks, and at the retreat at Gwen and Art's place on the Cape, we would decide on the proposed scheme so we could get preliminary schematic plans ready by the end of July. "Then we'll get bids from Epoch [the prefab builder that Art and Gwen preferred] and conventional builders," she said. "We'll pick three potential builders, take a look at their work, and the core group will get an opportunity to interview them."

Our core meetings had fallen into a familiar pattern. We'd start with a warm-up intended to help us get to know one another better. For example, we'd go around the room, following the facilitator's instructions to "tell us something good that happened to you last week." Then we would have committee reports. Viv would give a treasurer's report and Art would give the big financial picture. Either Art or Carla would let us know how our quest for subsidized units was coming along. Joan would introduce new members and review our demographics. Someone from the DOC would give a report. Then we would have an exercise in which we would grapple with a particular question.

After the June 23 meeting, many of us walked the few blocks from the Friends Meeting House to Sheila's house for a design committee meeting. It was a warm evening and the sun was touching the horizon as we took seats on her back deck. Bruce, the architect that Art and Gwen had hired, tacked alternate plans on the trunks of surrounding trees. We discussed the pros and cons of each. Then we came to the question of elevators. At that time, we were planning to have thirty-eight units. The question was, how we would get that number?

Instead of drafting several alternate plans showing three or four different possibilities, as Gwen often did when we had a major decision to make, she presented only one plan: one four-story building with an elevator, two sets of "stacked flats" (three-story buildings without elevators and with a unit on each side of a central staircase), and several town houses. Gwen wanted our approval for the stacked flats, which would be walk-ups and thus departed from our vision of a community accessible to all.

Several of us questioned whether walk-ups were a mistake; people could have difficulty due to handicaps or age. Someone responded, "Older people can choose to live in the common house with the elevator." Barbara says she and several others pointed out that "anyone, regardless of age, can break a leg, have a debilitating illness, be pregnant." "I carried my two babies up three flights in the South End and it didn't hurt me one bit," said Florence.

I don't remember speaking up, but I do remember that I had many thoughts: We shouldn't be building inaccessible units; it contradicts our mission. I should say something, but it will be hard to buck Gwen. If I speak in favor of total accessibility, I will likely suffer failure and antagonism. It will not affect my unit because I'm planning to choose a town house.

We spent most of the time at the next core group meeting, held on June 30, planning the site, with Gwen and Bruce presenting bubble diagrams to show us various possibilities. Once more we discussed elevators, and this time there was strong support for them and strong opposition. While I sat silently, a groundswell against more than one elevator developed: They cost too much; they were isolating; they would detract from community. Assuming that the Americans with Disabilities Act would force us to have elevators in all of our multiple-unit buildings, I decided not to buck the tide. It turned out I was wrong. The act does not cover buildings that are three stories or less, and the stacked flats were three stories tall.

At our second weekend at Art and Gwen's place on the Cape, July 13 and 14, Bruce and Gwen did what they often did, offering a number of options, but had not done about elevators. They presented nine site sketches showing different ways to handle parking (aboveground at either end of the site, underground, or covered), with different costs and different amounts of room for greenery and outdoor recreation. We decided to put the parking underground in order to have more green space, even though that would cost more.

To make up for that, we decided to have forty-one units instead of thirty-eight, reasoning that since we had so many single-person households, we wouldn't be that much larger than other cohousing communities. (The going wisdom, first put forward by Jan Gudmand-Høyer, the architect who invented cohousing in Denmark, was that twenty to thirty units was the best size for a cohousing community.) We also discussed storage. Gwen warned, "Storage space is not cheap. In-unit space is better; things stored out of unit are often forgotten."

Art announced that we now had enough money to buy the land and could use the exemption process to try to get diversity. Then we had a long discussion about how to attract families, and Betsy volunteered to head a task force. She and Charles asked for a refund of their deposit if we could not get twelve families with children.

Barbara reported on her survey, although many of us had not yet filled out ours. The strongest themes were social belonging, social commitment, loneliness, personal growth, a safe place to experiment with new and rewarding behaviors, enthusiasm for this experiment, learning from others, and multigenerational relationships. Many responders noted the special skills they could contribute. Several offered conflict-resolution skills, but only one thought she or he might need that kind of help.

We had dinner, followed by an evening of singing and games, while tropical storm Bertha raged outside. Frank and David taught Art and me how to play backgammon, and Lyn began work on a needlepoint of two cats in front of a bookcase, which she said would take her four years to finish. Someone said we'd be in our new homes long before she finished.

The next day after breakfast, we gathered for a group photo on the porch. Then there was a meeting of the family task force while Art, David, and Ted put up a clothesline and I tried to cut back the same mulberry bush I had attacked the year before. My goal was to give the hydrangea behind it enough sun to grow. David came by and we chatted about the intense blue of Cape Cod hydrangeas. He said he thought it looked artificial and I said I liked it. In the afternoon, some of us went to the beach and then we all went home.

At the meeting two weeks later (July 28), Art presented an agreement that would allow some households to make smaller down payments. Carla objected to the clause that Betsy and Charles had asked for that would allow a household to drop out and have their down payment refunded if we were not able to attract twelve families with children. Carla pointed out that we were not permitting members to drop out and receive a full refund if we did not meet our other diversity goals, such as those concerning race and age, and that making refunds on the basis of a single diversity issue was beyond the scope of the finance committee. I agreed with her and pointed out that it would give households that were given exemptions rights to refunds that households that made the full down payment were not receiving. In order for us to get more families with children, we would have to depend on the families we already had to work hard to use their contacts to attract more families. Art said the finance committee would review that clause.

Two dueling handouts were presented at the next meeting. They underlined the difference between building a standard condo and building a cohousing community. One, titled "Status of Progress in Cambridge Cohousing Design," was Gwen's. It listed the decisions she and Bruce believed to be "firm" and those they believed to be "in process or not yet addressed." The other, authored by Betsy and first presented on our Listserv, was titled "Design Decisions: Process and Timetable." Without being specific about which decisions she had in mind, Betsy declared that she was "concerned by the lack of clarity . . . regarding when, how, and by whom key design decisions are being made." She proposed four changes. First, Oaktree, Art and Gwen's company, should create and distribute a three-month timetable with the dates when key decisions needed to be made; second, each issue requiring a decision should be discussed at a core group meeting; third, Oaktree should provide descriptive materials regarding each issue to be decided and present them at least one meeting before the decision needed to be made; and, finally, key decisions should follow the "regular consensus decision-making process adopted by the CCH LLP."

A number of emails followed. Florence was a lawyer, and, like others, she volunteered her special skills. She pointed out that asking Oaktree to work with a design committee was "contrary to our agreement with them that they would work with a single Development Oversight Committee" and that "perhaps Oaktree would be willing to add another committee if we could significantly cut the amount of design work having to be done in the general meeting." However, she noted: "We run into a problem here, since many people are unwilling to accept recommendations from either Oaktree or any committee on the matters now being decided that they consider personally important. We tried 'design committees,' but it didn't work because everyone wanted to be on THE Design Committee, which is how it became a Committee of the whole." She suggested that, when the plans were more complete and people knew where their unit would be, maybe subcommittees devoted to particular issues would work. "But," she added, "I bet you no one will be willing to allow a small committee to decide on the color of the siding!"

Betsy replied on August 23:

> I was (and am) unwilling to accept major recommendations from Oaktree (or, for that matter, from any individual or couple) that are not first digested by a committee or through a general discussion. I would, however, be willing to accept design recommendations coming through a committee if I felt that it was really functioning "as a committee." The design committee meetings I've been to have been loose presentations, mostly by Gwen and Bruce, . . . not good forums for reviewing and critiquing proposals or brainstorming alternative solutions. I'd like to see a design committee run by a chairperson, with a pre-announced agenda so folks with particular concerns could come when appropriate. . . . If the committee functioned well, . . . I think the core group would usually accept them. Personally, I would be only too happy to avoid a discussion about the color of siding :-)! I guess I'd kind of hope it wasn't *beige,* but honestly, if people who know more about this subject and have thought it through told me beige was the best choice, and why, I'd be glad to accept it.

Betsy's complaints and call for reform were a response to a pattern that was becoming common: Gwen's tendency to hire subcontractors and make decisions much as she had always done as a developer of ordinary condos. Her experience was in the housing market, where she acted in terms of reciprocity and opposing roles. Even though she was a member of the group, a fellow commoner who should have been pooling with the rest of us, her relations with us were contractual and reciprocal. On the one side were the people she called "the professionals," which included herself and all the subcontractors she hired. On the other side were the rest of us.

Gwen was sure that there was a simpler way to build cohousing. Shortly after our buildings were complete and we were all moved in, she set about to prove her point. On a piece of land she bought at the corner of our block, she developed a multiple-unit building the way she thought cohousing should be constructed—professionally, by a builder, the way any other multiunit building is constructed, with the one difference that she hired a cohousing consultant to guide those to whom she sold units. Her building stands at our corner, a nice condominium, like any other nice condominium. But it is not cohousing. Its residents do not form a community; they do not share meals regularly; they do not accompany each other to the hospital when there is an emergency; they do not live with the comfort that right outside their door there are friends ready to help when help is needed; they do not celebrate each other's birthdays; in short, they are neighbors because they live next door to each other, but they have never become commoners who share their commons; there is no sense that they form a community. Like any other condo development, it has a board that manages the property and its residents greet each other politely when they pass in the street. Several developers have tried to create cohousing by completing the building and selling units to residents as cohousing. So far, it has not worked.

Charles Durrett, the cohousing developer and a coauthor of *Cohousing: A Contemporary Approach to Housing Ourselves,* tried to establish a certification process for cohousing that would work like the organic farming certification process. If it were adopted, a development would have to meet special criteria to be legitimately called cohousing. Participation was first on Chuck's list of criteria. Cohousing should be co-developed, co-designed, and co-organized with the future resident group. According to Chuck, genuine participation along the way is necessary because it creates a culture of decision making together. During the building process, strangers get to know and care about each other and become friends as they build their homes together.

Gwen conducted the DOC meetings not as a group of equals coming together to make mutually beneficial decisions, but as the opposing sides in a contractual relationship. She came prepared with the agenda, which always included at least two items: a progress report on construction and a list of the checks that needed to be signed. Occasionally, as she did when deciding where to park our cars, she came to the group with several plans from which to choose. Often, though, her request for collaboration came without alternatives and when it was too late to make a different choice without added expense, as happened when she decided to build the two stacked flats without elevators.

Florence, who facilitated the social organization committee, which had made many stabs at developing procedures, announced that the committee was throwing in the towel. The committee had met to consider a bill of rights, she said, but decided we had too much other work at this stage to be able to pay attention to that. They suggested that members collect ideas for discussion at future meetings about "general behavior, civility, interaction, conflict (clearness in), mechanisms for resolution, and need for training, 'group speak,' food preferences, pets, drugs legal and illegal, shared responsibilities, commitment to responsibilities, and to do a fair share of work." As for socializing, she said, "at this point with so much planning to do, our socializing occurs mostly in committee meetings." She said that she had spent more time recently in meetings than with her other friends. It looked as though for Florence, at least, our work to make us less lonely was making us more so.

We were just months from the enthusiasm and optimism that had followed our signing of the contract with Gwen and Art and our purchase of the land, but we were up against problems faced by many cohousing communities. Rob Sandelin, a wise and frequent contributor to Cohousing-L, the national cohousing Listserv, put his finger on the problem when he wrote, "Community is created to enhance relationships. This is the point of cohousing." The problem is that in order to "create a place to live in community . . . cohousers become real estate developers and . . . real estate development often requires processes that run counter to relationship building." He added that "almost always, relationship building falls to the wayside in deference to real estate development issues because of money concerns." If that happens, "if your development process is damaging your relationships, then you are out of balance with your purpose."

His was another way of stating the difference between Erikson's poles on a culture's axis of variation; Sahlin's pooling and reciprocity; a market and a common; and the effect of markets and commons on relationships and on loneliness. It was easy in those days to fall out of balance with our purpose. Yes, we wanted a community, a common, a place where we would have many friends and be less lonely, but we also wanted to move into our private homes, our units, as quickly and inexpensively as possible. To get our homes, we needed to stay on the fast track and keep our prices down. And we had to do that with only a vague idea of where our units would be, what our units would look like, and what they would cost.

Five

The Developers Take Over—
Full Steam Ahead
Fall 1996

Now we needed to choose our units. At a meeting in August, before the unit prices were firmly set, we had our first selection. It was a casual affair. We milled around and chatted as we looked over a board listing all the units. Each household put its lottery number in a first-choice column for one unit and in a second-choice column for another. By that time, I had decided against a town house and my first choice was a three-bedroom unit on the top floor of the common house. It was smaller than I wanted and it didn't have the private house feel of a town house, but it suited my other needs: accessibility no matter what might happen to me, the possibility of skylights, enough rooms for a study, a bedroom, and a guest room (although the last was not absolutely necessary, as the common house would have two guest rooms). My second choice was a small town house. We would make our final choices in December, after an appraiser had set the prices for each of the units.

At the August 18 core meeting, Gwen announced that we had had a successful gathering of neighbors at the site. Gwen and Bruce presented site diagrams, and our future neighbors were generally positive. Most of their concerns were about parking. Gwen added that some trains came by during the presentation, "but we hardly noticed them." We had been worrying about the noise of trains ever since we considered buying our site, which sat between the tracks of the commuter train going out to Concord and Acton, Massachusetts, and a narrow street with only one lane for moving traffic when cars were parked on both sides of the street, which they always were.

The late-August newsletter announced that final deposits had to be sent to Viv by September 10 at the latest. There was a full-page column that listed meetings till the end of December, mostly those of the the the core group whose name had been changed to the "General," which met weekly at first and then biweekly on Sundays, and the DOC, which met weekly on Tuesdays. There were also meetings of the finance, steering, design, and membership committees. Probably in response to Betsy's demand, Gwen supplied a list of milestones: the submission of a special permit; the date all deposits would be due; the first hearing on the special permit; the closing; and the second hearing on the special permit. In the fall, I moved back to Connecticut and Don took over the newsletter.

As summer cools into fall each year, the Cambridge Arts Council runs a festival along the banks of the Charles River, which flows between Cambridge and Boston. There's lots of music (jazz, folk, and world), food, dancing, and crafts. At the 1996 festival, Carla and Viv sat at a table and handed out flyers about Cambridge Cohousing. Not long afterward, the *Globe* printed a story about our development. With all that publicity, our worries about attracting enough members were over: About 125 people came to our next orientation meeting on September 15.

That same day, we added two couples, bringing our membership to twelve singles, six families with kids, and six couples. We were also planning a two-unit residence for four developmentally challenged men and their helper. Altogether, that brought us up to forty-one adults in twenty-six households. We still had fourteen units available; but with all the people who showed up in response to the *Globe* story, we were not too worried about being able to fill them. We were about to make our final payment on the land. Art said our construction would be within the $6.1 million budget and that the total cost of the project would be $8,529,000. With down payments and large loans from some members, we had more than $1.7 million and could easily close on the land and start building. We planned to get a construction loan for 75 percent of the building costs.

At the end of September, after Bruce had been working on our project all summer, Art sent a letter to members, strongly urging us not to issue an RFP (request for proposals) to architects and contractors as Florence had promised in her early report from the DOC, but instead to hire Bruce, who, Art said, "has a good working relationship with a well-qualified modular manufacturer[Epoch]." Moreover, he argued, "we believe that using a modular approach to construction will create higher quality housing at a lower cost," achieving "projected savings in a range between $250,000 and $750,000." He also pointed out that "producing a standard set of working drawings and negotiating a non-modular (conventional) construction contract would delay the project by at least six months, during which time the group would be paying interest on the loans used to purchase the land." Art further promised that "[i]f the Members accept a recommendation from the Development Oversight Committee to hire Bruce, an AIA contract with Bruce would be written which includes input from the Design Committee regarding all design issues including but not limited to common areas, landscaping, and the general appearance of the building (the style). Also, input into the design of each Member's unit will be consistent with the Development Agreement."

At the September 29 meeting, we had a visit from Don Lindemann, editor of the national cohousing magazine. Only twelve full members were at the meeting, and we had thirty-five guests. The twelve did not make up a quorum; nevertheless, we made many decisions. We decided to pay the Cambridge Friends Meeting for letting us use their facilities for our meetings; to accept modifications to our LLP (mostly about when payments were due); and we agreed to replace Sheila, who had to leave the group, with Gerard on the DOC. To celebrate our acquisition of the land, we had a ceremony with a big group hug and a little glitter house representing cohousing brought by Carla (probably left over from her last Christmas celebration). Barbara distributed a three-page analysis of the pros and cons of forming as a co-op or as a condominium, and we made plans for a meeting on October 7 to present the benefits of Epoch and heat pumps. During the first weekend in October, some of us attended an East Coast Cohousing Conference.

Mark Kelly, our HVAC (heating, ventilation, and air-conditioning) contractor, came to our next meeting. With the same simple reasoning that characterized the presentation of most decisions, Barbara introduced him, saying, "Mark Kelly will explain how to spend a little more now to save money over the long run." Following Mark's explanation, we all agreed that we wanted a geothermal heat pump system that would circulate water through three deep wells to use the constant earth temperature of about fifty-five degrees to heat us in winter and cool us in summer. It would cost more to build and install, but promised to save us money and save the Earth's resources in the long run. We also went along with Art's recommendation to hire Bruce and have our buildings fabricated at Epoch's factory in New Hampshire.

On October 15, we presented our plans to the Cambridge Planning Board. The meeting was attended by a dozen of us and about twice as many of our future neighbors. No one spoke against our plans, but neighbors did present concerns about parking, traffic, and garbage disposal. At the October 16 general meeting, Gwen announced that Carl Goldberg of CM Construction and Bruce were under contract. She also announced that we had owned our

Richdale Avenue site for a week. She said there were no toxins on the site.

Gwen thought we needed a little ceremony to mark our acquisition of the site, so she read a piece about Native Americans who had lived on our site, feasting on its produce. She said we should think for a minute about our community-to-be, and then she presented a bowlful of soil from all parts of the site and carried it around the circle, placing a scoop of dirt into each person's cupped hands. She then went around the circle once more, this time gathering the handfuls of soil back into the bowl. Florence followed with a bowl of water to wash the dirt off our hands and a towel to dry them. Gwen said the soil in the bowl would be mixed later with more soil for a fruit tree we would plant.

Next, we had to answer the question of whether we would be organized as a co-op or as a condo. Once more, Barbara presented the pros and cons of each. Someone who never did become a member said that a co-op would structurally promote community, while a condo would structurally promote individualism. It was, he said, the difference between socialism and capitalism. It was rare to hear anyone using those terms, or naming any of our choices in broad political, economic, or social terms. He was, of course, talking about pooling our resources to create a commons, a community. But instead, we chose to structure ourselves as a condo, mostly for the greater ease of getting mortgages from banks that favored condos and the tax benefits of a condo and because those favoring the condo claimed that as a co-op we would not receive the residential exemption in Cambridge real estate taxes that each resident owner of a condo would receive. Although that was not correct, no one questioned it, and with seventeen green cards and two people—I was one of them—raising a yellow card to show serious reservations, but no red card to block the decision, we decided to become a condo, not a co-op. As Rob Sandelin had said, "almost always, relationship building falls to the wayside in deference to real estate development issues because of money concerns."

In terms of the market or the commons, we had chosen for the market. That choice limited our ability to vet new members, something a co-op would have permitted. As a condo association, new members would only be required to meet the seller's price; they would not have to know anything about cohousing. As the years went by and some of the original members sold their units and were replaced by new owners, that hardly mattered most of the time. New owners would arrive, eager to be a part of our cohousing community. But occasionally new owners would be surprised to learn that there was any difference between Cambridge Cohousing and an ordinary condo. The seller of a unit, or the real estate agent, eager for a quick sale at the highest-possible price, did not even tell the buyer that the unit was part of a special cohousing community. Then it would take some time and negotiation, which sometimes didn't work, to encourage the new owner to be part of the community. Had we been organized as a co-op, all that would have been taken care of as buyers were vetted.

On October 20, Florence explained another distinction, one that probably would make no difference in ordinary condos but would make a difference for us: the difference between condo by-laws, which need to be boilerplate in order to get mortgages, and condo rules and regulations, which banks hardly look at and could be more specific about how we would manage ourselves. For that reason, we would put most of our agreements into our rules and regulations.

Also, Joan explained about Glen, their son, who would be one of the men in the special-needs unit. She suggested that we form a task force or liaison group between the special-needs unit and the rest of the community. Then Jeff presented a proposal on committees that Don had drawn up, pointing out that these were just operating principles.

Betsy was concerned about being required to participate, but she and anyone else who was worried was assured that no one would be required to do anything; there would be no fines nor other means of enforcement; no one was imposing anything on us—all participation would be totally voluntary. This would not be the last time that the question of whether the community would agree to require everyone to contribute in some manner to the community was raised. Usually, the question would be brushed off, often by David, who was quick to assure the questioner that we would never require a contribution or a commitment to the community. Around the country, most cohousing communities do stipulate that a certain amount of time, usually four hours a month, be given to the community. But few communities have any means of enforcement.

Here again we ran into the misconception that commons are without management or rules. No commons could last very long without rules and some means of enforcement. That was Elinor Ostrom's central observation. She studied hundreds of commons and in 2009 won the Nobel Prize in Economics for her analysis. In her central work, she listed eight principles for the successful management of a commons. Two of the eight principles were to "develop a system carried out by community members, for monitoring members' behavior" and "use graduated sanctions for rule violators." (Ostrom 2015, 90) Many times over the years, some of us would try to deal with the fact that a handful of members did nothing for the community. Then in 2017, a committee called the Values Circle developed a list of values that was adopted by the community. They included "engaging equitably through our care, time and work in our community while recognizing that individuals contribute in many ways" and "being reliable members who commit to and follow through on the work that needs to be done." Now, people who are considering buying a unit are shown the list and once every year we have a brief ceremony when members are asked to make a commitment to those values. Despite that, a handful of members do nothing for the community and the rest of us have no idea what to do about it.

With the influx following the *Globe* article, Joan announced that there were twenty-eight families that wanted to become members, but we had only twelve units left. We had twelve singles and only six families, so in order to meet our plan to have thirteen singles, thirteen families with children under fifteen, and thirteen households with two or more members and one wild card, we decided not to accept any more singles.

Back in New Haven, working at preparing my classes and finishing my book, I was pretty much cut off from the project. I tried to travel up on weekends as often as I could, both to visit my sons and to attend meetings. My coho lifeline was the newsletter that Don was publishing almost single-handedly. He was also trying to whip a committee structure into shape. The early-November newsletter was a testament to his efforts. It contained the charters from our six committees. It also had announcements of our progress. The most important milestone was that the Cambridge Planning Board had approved our application for a special permit. Once more, Gwen had shown her prowess. The board liked our plans to put parking underground and to build only forty-one units, rather than the fifty-three we could have built on the site. The next hurdle would be to get a building loan.

At the November 7 general meeting, we agreed by consensus to the following: to give Carla five hundred dollars to seek funding for affordable units; that we would use gas for our hot water and our common kitchen stove, but there would be no gas, which some members considered a fire hazard, in our units; and that our windows would be double-hung ones (cheaper) except for the windows facing the tracks, which would be casement. We left the decision of fireplaces in the units for a later time. There was strong sentiment for only one in the common living room, but Gwen argued, successfully, as it turned out, to allow fireplaces in the town houses and top-floor units in the common house and stacked flats.

Now that we had decided to be a condo, where each unit would be privately owned, not a co-op, we still had to decide whether there would be any limits on profit taking. I, Barbara, and several others argued in favor, pointing out that there was value in our efforts to create cohousing that should stay with the community and that we didn't want to become an elite community. But there was strong opposition, mostly from those who argued that sellers would need funds for their new homes. A special task force was formed to address the question. Its members came back with three plans. One plan would restrict profit taking to a certain percentage each year. Another, the one I favored, would have calculated how much our original prices were below market value (because we did not use brokers and there was no investor's profit) and then preserved that savings for the community, at least during our first five years. The third plan was to place no limitation on profit taking. Only the third plan reached consensus, once again favoring our private interests over those of our community. The community's only way to affect sales would be to have a strong and current waiting list and a right of first refusal.

The minutes of the general meeting on November 17 announced that a garage on the site was coming down, that Epoch would start building our boxes in January and would deliver them in the spring, that construction would begin soon at the west end, and that Art and Gwen were planning a vacation for two weeks in the rain forest of Ecuador. We agreed to start meetings at 3:00 P.M. to make it easier for families with children. The design committee divided into groups, concentrating on various rooms in the common house. I was on the library committee with Barbara and Bob. Bruce presented two schemes for the common house and announced a finish fair for the following day. At the finish fair, we would decide on bathroom and kitchen fixtures and appliances, flooring, lighting, and whether we wanted a fireplace in our units.

The late-November newsletter announced that the East Cambridge Savings Bank would give us a construction loan. A groundbreaking ceremony was scheduled for December 1. Gwen said we should each bring a shovel. After the groundbreaking, we would meet to make our final choice of units. We had our final plans, and the appraiser's figures for all the units would soon be available.

That newsletter also had a report from a task force formed by the community committee to create a conflict and conflict resolution committee. Deb, its first facilitator, wrote that "because we are interconnected, problems and conflicts of many types will impact directly or indirectly upon the community. Some exist now in our cohousing community which urgently needs a procedure to enable the community to attend to them, address and resolve them." The report included a list of people who might serve on the committee, and included the background each nominee would bring to the committee. I was gratified to see my name on the list of twenty-three, with the qualities that I was "a sociologist, sensible, and had a broad perspective," but I was troubled that a major qualification for six of the people on the list was that they were familiar with "Quaker ways" of clarity and resolution. No other members were considered suitable for the committee on the basis of their religion.

December 1 was a dark, drizzly, chilly day. We gathered with our shovels at our site for the groundbreaking ceremony. Some of us read poems we had written for the occasion. We ate doughnuts and drank cider, and the kids ran around in the mud. Then we went to the Friends Meeting House to choose our units.

By that time, the plans were pretty well set, as were the prices for our units. The main building, a four-story structure that would have an elevator, would be our common house and would have common facilities in its basement and on most of its first floor.

These would include the children's room, kitchen, dining room, living room, mail room, entrance lobby, teen room, storage room, rec room, garage, bike room, and electrical and mechanical rooms for our heating and cooling facilities. There would be a studio unit, a one-bedroom, a two-bedroom, a three-bedroom, and a four-bedroom unit on the second, third, and fourth floors. On the first, there would also be two units with two bedrooms. Then there were the three-story stacked flats—one at the east end and the other at the west end. The one on the east end would have a two-bedroom and a three-bedroom unit on each floor. The one in the west end would house the special-needs unit and the helper unit on the first floor and have a three-bedroom and a four-bedroom flat on each of the two floors above that. There were also five small town houses and seven large ones.

From the time of our first drawing for units, several members had dropped out and several others had joined, putting my number 20 at about the midpoint of the twenty-nine members who would choose. Each of us was given one small sticker dot with our lottery number on it. One by one, we went up to the chart with all the units listed on it and pasted our dot by the unit we wanted. There was also a newsprint pad on an easel where we could write down our comments and problems. After everyone had chosen units, we took our seats in the large circle to discuss problems.

Francesca was close to tears when she told us, "I always said that the next place I would live, my father would be able to visit. He can't climb stairs. By the time I got to choose, there were no units in the common house that we could afford and no ground-floor units in the stacked flats. We've sold our house; we can't go back. I don't know what we will do." Deb said, "I know what Francesca means; I have a mother-in-law who can't climb stairs. I don't want to live in a place she can't visit." Once again, I was silent. My number was lower than Francesca's, so I was able to choose a unit in the common house, with an elevator. I, too, had decided I would never again live in a place that someone could not reach in a wheelchair. That was years ago, when our friend Roy, a polio victim, came to see our new home in New Haven and our sons had to carry him up the stairs in his wheelchair. He seemed frightened and humiliated.

Over the next few days, emails flew. The first message was a long one from Jeff, who said that he had not spoken up on that fateful summer evening when we decided to have the two stacked flats without elevators because he and Deb had just joined the group and were provisional members. He compared elevators in the stacked flats to the children's room and said that if we were willing to pay for the children's room so that we could attract children, we should be willing to pay for the elevators in the stacked flats so that all our units would be accessible to everyone.

At the next design committee meeting, most of the planned agenda was scrapped so that the ten or so members there could discuss our accessibility problem. Most thought that a mistake had been made and that it needed to be corrected as inexpensively as possible. By that time, our plans were completed and building was under way. Any change would be expensive. The ideal solution, if feasible, would be to put elevators in the stacked flat buildings. Barbara, the facilitator of the design committee, agreed to convey the tenor of the meeting to Gwen.

The least expensive solution, Gwen responded, would be to add stair chairs to the two sets of stacked flats. That would entail widening both stairways by two feet to make way for the stair chairs. At the time, it seemed a reasonable solution, but it was a decision many of us would regret for years to come. Stair chairs did not really make units in the upper floors of the stacked flats accessible. What we did not imagine then, but would know in the years to come, was that someone confined to a wheelchair could not visit a third-floor unit in one of the stacked flats. She would have to get from her wheelchair to the bench on the chair stair, take the chair stair up to the second floor while someone carried her wheelchair up the first flight of stairs, then get back into her wheelchair to go down the long hall and start the whole process again to get from the second floor to the third.

I've often thought about that mistake. At the time, we did have one member confined to a wheelchair, but neither he nor his wife spoke up. The rest of us lacked the imagination to know that stair chairs could not really substitute for elevators. Often it is hard to imagine another point of view or how one's position might seem wrong by another moral or value standard. For example, when Florence argued against elevators, she was proud to boast that she had carried her two babies up three flights of stairs. At that moment, it probably did not even cross her mind that others, not lucky enough to be blessed with her strength, health, and vigor, might find those stairs impassable with or without a baby or two in their arms. Years later, plagued by a painful back disease, Florence would move from her flat on the third floor of one of the stacked flats to a unit in the common house, which did have an elevator.

Deciding whether all our members would be able to visit all the units was, for our small community, the moral equivalent of deciding whether all public buildings must be wheelchair-accessible. It was not until the question of accessibility had to be faced on an individual level that two of our members spoke out forcefully and we had to revisit our design. Even though most cohousers across the country consider themselves liberals, when it came to keeping all our units accessible or making all our units a bit less expensive, we chose the latter. For me, it brought back the day I was interviewing corporation managers for my dissertation. They were almost unanimously opposed to government aid of any kind—Medicare, Medicaid, TAFDC (Transitional Aid to Families with Dependent Children, otherwise known as welfare). You name it. If the program helped people not as lucky or, as they put it, "not as hardworking" as they were, they opposed it. Only the ones whose life paths put them or people they loved in a situation where some sort of extra help was needed (dialysis, a new home after a tornado had blown down the one they were living in) could any of them see the benefit of these programs. Thus, one manager, whose mother needed an expensive operation, thought Medicare was a good program; another, whose child suffered renal failure, praised the special assistance Medicare gives such patients. "A transplant is so expensive," she said, "we would not have been able to afford it; our son would have died."

It takes a certain kind of blindness to set out to create a community open to all and then to build places in that community that some members of the community cannot visit. On that beautiful August evening, we were blind visionaries. It took a couple of months for our mistake to begin to hit home and make some of us realize what we had done. If Jeff and I thought about the disjuncture between our vision of diversity and our plans for accessibility, we said nothing until Deb, Jeff's wife, realized that the only units available by the time they could put their dot on a unit would be inaccessible to his mother. Like the corporation manager's wife, the problem had to hit home and become personal before he would speak up.

The vision and the blindness represent the two poles on the axis of variation that rock our contemporary world. Like us, most people hold both the vision and the blindness. It is finding their balance in our lives, in our communities, in our governments, indeed in our world, that is difficult. On the one pole are individual rights, the pursuit of happiness and wealth, capitalism, the striving for and achieving individual excellence, and our pride in our achievements, whether it is the ability to carry our babies up three flights of stairs, getting into Harvard, or living in a beautiful home. At the opposite pole are our commons, our public parks, schools, and roads, the natural resources none of us owns and all of us use, and building a community accessible to all. Almost all of our politics represent a choice between these two value systems, and almost all of the tears and trials at CCH were over the choices we had to make between them.

Sometimes, even though our whole point in working together was to create community, we would come down on the side of individual rights. Sometimes we would favor the community. And sometimes we would find a compromise. In the case of the eight inaccessible units in the two stacked-flat buildings, many of us thought we had found a compromise. We widened the staircases and put in stair chairs. Some of us congratulated ourselves on a problem well solved.

Over time, others, I among them, saw those stair chairs as a mistake made more than once as we paid again and again to have them repaired, and watched as one owner after another was forced by illness and disability to move from units on the second and third floors of the stacked flats to units in the elevator building. Fortuitous timing had allowed Florence and two others who began their coho days in a stacked flat to move to the elevator building when physical problems made climbing stairs difficult. Not surprising is the higher rate of turnover in the stacked flats: Of the seventeen units in the common house, fourteen were still owned in 2016 by people who were members of the community in 1997. Of the eight units on the second and third floors of the stacked flats, only three were owned in 2016 by people who were members of the community in 1997. Two of the original members had left the community and three had been able to move to the common house. The compromise of installing stair chairs helped those who had a temporary disability, such as someone who was recovering from knee-replacement surgery, but it still forced those with a permanent disability or with friends or relatives with permanent disabilities or in need of wheelchairs to solve their accessibility problem individually and privately.

December 1, 1996, was a dark, drizzly, chilly day. We gathered with our shovels at our site for our ground-breaking ceremony. PHOTOS BY EDWARD A. MASON.

The first task was to clear the land. We were surprised to find a mower on the roof of the garage.

Watching the crane lift and place modules in March-April was pretty dramatic entertainment.

The modules arrived as oversize truckloads.
PHOTO BY EDWARD A. MASON.

It would take many meetings to create a commons. Food and flowers helped; so did name tags as we were getting to know each other.
PHOTOS COURTESY OF CAMBRIDGE COHOUSING.

One of three cranes that set the modules in place.

The author, holding umbrella center, Ed Mason, and many other cohousers in front of their just-completed front entrance. PHOTO COURTESY OF CAMBRIDGE COHOUSING.

Some of the last modules sit on the future Pretty Great Lawn, waiting to be fitted into place. PHOTO COURTESY OF CAMBRIDGE COHOUSING.

Before the boxes could be lifted into place, they had to be backed onto the site. Not easy from the narrow street with traffic and parking in both directions. PHOTO BY EDWARD A. MASON.

Residents cutting and moving planks of wood. In those days we only masked if we were sensitive to sawdust! PHOTO BY EDWARD A. MASON.

Community painting the fence (proof that Viv helped paint the fence!).
PHOTO BY EDWARD A. MASON.

Children playing
near the future
vegetable gardens.
PHOTO COURTESY
OF CAMBRIDGE
COHOUSING.

Planting trees. This
tree grew tall!
PHOTO BY EDWARD
A. MASON.

Bringing a homemade cake to the contractors. Maybe sweets would speed things up!
PHOTO BY EDWARD A. MASON.

Planning the vegetable garden. "The garlic should go over there."
PHOTO BY EDWARD A. MASON.

Six

We Choose Our Units

January 1997

January 5, 1997, was the date set for our final choice of units. I wasn't there. Every year no matter what else we did, Dick and I would review all our New Year's Eves together. Most years, we were with friends. Some New Year's Eves were so special that I can still remember them all by myself. There was the year Harry was born and our upstairs neighbor came down to celebrate and help us soothe our colicky baby. The next year, our friends Joan and Roy's first baby was born and Dick went to the hospital with Roy. Dick came home, marveling at the power of love. "There she was on the other side of the glass all red and wrinkly like any baby, but tears were rolling down Roy's face and all he could say was, 'Isn't she beautiful?'" Another year, we went with a bunch of Brooklyn Heights friends to see *Die Fledermaus* at the Met and then came back to a cork-popping party.

By 1997, with no one to help me remember our past New Year's Eves, I stopped trying. The trick was to get through the holidays without feeling too lonely. Taking a tour was one way. So on January 5, 1997, the day set for our third and final choice of units, I was on a tour in the jungles of the Amazon. Ralph had agreed to be my proxy. He knew that my first choice was the three-bedroom flat on the top floor of the common house; Viv, who had drawn a lower number than I, said she might choose that unit. Before I left for my trip, Jeff, who with Deb had joined late and therefore had a higher number than I did, called to find out if I would be choosing that unit. I felt bad to be preventing them from having it, but I said that if Viv didn't choose it before me, that would be my choice. If Viv did choose that unit, I was going to choose one of the small town houses, though I thought it would be pretty dark with only north and south windows and larger buildings shading its south side. I had to have a third choice, but I can't remember what it was. I really wanted that fourth-floor three-bedroom unit.

All day on January 5, I waited for Ralph's call; it didn't come. After a sleepless night, I put in a call to him. He said he was sorry he hadn't called the day before, but when the meeting had finally ended, it was after 10:00 P.M. and he thought that was too late to call. "Why did it take so long?" I asked. "Ellen couldn't decide which unit she wanted," he said. "And me," I asked, "what unit did I get?" "The one you wanted," he said offhandedly. I thanked him, shared my good news with a family that was on the tour with me, and jumped into the hotel pool.

The early-January issue of our newsletter carried a page-and-a-half "Development Report" from Gwen. It was sober but upbeat.

> If we have a finance commitment from a bank by then, we should be able to be digging foundations and setting concrete forms at the end of the month. Epoch will start putting modules together in New Hampshire at the same time. We're really very close to starting, and construction will proceed remarkably quickly once it starts. (Anticipate watching the crane lift and place modules by March-April: it is pretty dramatic entertainment!) We are currently expecting that move-ins in the East End will start in mid-summer

(June/July) followed by the Common House occupancy. We should
all be moved in by September or October at the latest. We have
gotten back our revised appraisal, which makes the case that the
project as currently designed will be worth $9,700,000 or roughly
$1,000,000 more than the project is projected to cost.

All Gwen wanted from us was to have our full 30 percent deposits
ready on time. She concluded by saying, "Even though this group
is putting in amazing hours these days, I frequently marvel at the
enthusiasm that pervades our deliberations. We're really getting
there as a functioning community."

On the first page of the same newsletter, Bruce, our architect,
laid out the plans for our meetings with him. We had to choose
fixtures, appliances, floor coverings and other finishes, and sign
off on our unit plans. Bruce thought it should take only an hour,
"although," he said, "I will meet with you for a second hour (at
additional cost) if necessary."

The February newsletter led off with the cheerful headline BIG
NEWS! CONSTRUCTION IS STARTING. The contractor had begun to
dig the foundation in Cambridge and construction of the prefabricated modules had begun in New Hampshire. With each newsletter,
Gwen published a graphic that charted our progress. The February
chart showed final completion and likely move-in by June 23, 1997.

Underlying the optimism, however, there was worry. Construction was already falling behind schedule and costs were rising. A
contract with the builder had been signed and now every alteration
in the plans became a "change order," that increased the cost of
the project. As Rob Sandelin had noted, cohousing is a mixture
of the private and the communal, but often the private trumps the
communal. We were all fulfilling the American dream of having
our own private home, our own little castle, and it was hard, as we
thought of our private dwellings, not to act like consumers out to
get as much as we could for as little as possible.

Reciprocity and special deals ruled as members asked for extras beyond the choice of fixtures, appliances, and floor coverings that the meetings with Bruce were supposed to be about. One person decided two balconies would be better than one; another wanted an extra washer and dryer hookup; a third thought building out a couple more feet in their bedroom, giving them a view of the sunset, would be great. The list of extras grew, and with it, the secrets. Hardly anybody knew what somebody else was getting—it was all between the unit owner and Bruce—or else we all would have been asking for the extras someone else got. I surely would have. When I learned about them several years later, I was unhappy that I hadn't known about the possibilities, for I, too, would have asked for a western view and an extra balcony, even if I would have had to pay extra for them. Like everyone else, I was trying to make my private property as good as I could afford it to be without even a thought about the community we were building.

A commons requires a common vision. Groups with a shared identity, religious groups, for example, but any group, even one as small as a family, with its yearly celebrations of Thanksgiving, Easter, Passover, Ramadan, or Christmas, meet regularly. Simply by gathering, if not more evocatively, they reiterate their oneness and their shared vision. Not until 2017 did the members of Cambridge Cohousing give more than the passing nod we had given at our second meeting to our vision statement and draft and consent to a new statement of values. We never did gather in groups small or large to explore our values to see where they overlapped and where they diverged, something Barbara had asked us to do. The two or three times that Carla, probably feeling that we weren't doing enough to build affordable units, suggested that we have a retreat to explore our values, Gwen quickly countered that our vision statement had already done that. Some of us noted that the vision statement was so broadly written that almost anyone could imagine their own dream reflected therein. Unlike a market, which needs only rules and some means of seeing to it that everybody follows them, a commons needs a sense of commonality, a language, a culture to hold the group together.

Exchanges and markets are made for difference, for being better than the next guy and showing it off. Conspicuous consumption—upscale SUVs, designer clothes, and elite schools are creations of markets. The commons is made for equality, for sharing, for everybody having what they need. There are no limits to markets; commons provide a floor below which no one can fall. Freedom, liberty, independence, privacy, and competition are values of the market, while equal opportunity and living sustainably are values of the commons.

As market values prevailed during the winter of 1997, special perks piled up and squeaky wheels slowed our progress. Delays became increasingly noticeable. We met in February to find the causes and suggest solutions. Too many change orders were at the top of the list. The remedy, we decided, was to urge the developers, the DOC, and Bruce to hold the line: There were to be no more individual calls to Epoch, Oaktree, or Bruce until he had submitted our final plans to the Cambridge Planning Board. In the next newsletter, Bruce complained that some of us were taking too much of his and his assistant Ann's time: "[Ann] actually has a life beyond cohousing, please try to respect that." Plans were still not complete when Gwen and Art went off to the Galapagos for a two-week vacation. Not long after, Bruce went sailing in the British Virgin Islands, leaving Ann to steer the ship in Cambridge. Barbara and Ted took off for Bermuda and the design committee pretty much shut down.

New people were still joining. February brought us applications from a single woman who was planning to adopt a child from China, from two empty-nest couples, and from a young couple with two kids. While some of us were getting to know one another, there were always a few people at our meetings whom I didn't recognize. We began the February 23 meeting like any group of strangers by going around the room introducing ourselves.

Tricky Timing:
Selling the Old Place to Buy the New One

I was still living in Connecticut, anxious to get to Cambridge but wanting to time my move so that my new place would be ready for me when I sold my old place. When she came back from the Gala-pagos, I called Gwen to find out when our units would be ready. She said June. "Are you sure?" I asked. "Yes," she replied, "I'm sure." That must have been what she was telling all those who would have to sell their old homes in order to have the down payment for their new ones. She was focused on a developer's more usual concern: whether owners would be ready with their down payments when their units were ready. As buyers don't usually come onto the scene until construction is nearly complete, she probably had no experience with anxious buyers who needed a place to live. Following Gwen's assurance, I put my New Haven house on the market.

A Developer's Prerogative: Hiring Subcontractors

Another aspect of development where community building and construction seemed at cross purposes centered on subcontractors. Acting like the developer she was used to being, Gwen hired friendly subcontractors whenever she thought we needed their services. Not only did Gwen know where all the buildable land in Cambridge lay; she was also an expert networker. For example, when she thought it was time to get firm prices for our units, she hired an appraiser she knew. We thought his prices failed to reflect our ideas of what might make one unit more valuable than another. We wanted differences in pricing to reflect such amenities as a southern exposure, a basement, proximity to the elevator, or a unit on an upper floor in the elevator building. So we signed a check for Gwen's appraiser and then formed a pricing task force that produced nearly a dozen spreadsheets as it worked through the summer of 1997 to set unit prices the community would consider fair.

The flak was louder when Gwen hired an interior design firm. Francesca, as facilitator of IDA (interior design and art committee), had already been shopping for dining room chairs and tables and bringing samples to meetings for us to choose from. She had also started a scrapbook for us to submit pictures of furniture we hoped to contribute to the common house from the larger homes we would be leaving. As we would not be buying furniture except for the dining room, none of us thought we needed an interior design firm and we balked when we learned that Gwen had already signed a contract to pay her interior designers eighteen thousand dollars—much more than the dining room chairs and tables would cost.

Gwen, who sometimes didn't seem to appreciate the differences between building a cohousing community that was creating a commons and developing an ordinary condo, defended her decision, saying that she had visited five or six cohousing communities and that their facilities were not much different from those in other condos. She claimed that hiring an interior design team was part of subcontractor hiring that was in our contract with Oaktree. We needed the expertise of interior designers, she claimed, and told us that "even the architect wants them on the team." Anyway, it was too late to change, as she had already signed a contract with them. We paid them, but we did not use their services. Francesca, in the ways of a commons, was contributing all her work voluntarily.

Finally, in March, with Bruce, Gwen, and Art back from their southern sojourns, building really got going. Our buildings' footprints were set, but we were still working out the details of the plans while the modules were being built up in New Hampshire. Gwen wrote in the March newsletter that "we all need each other's love, trust and support in keeping this great venture moving forward with as much care and grace as possible. We're challenged by deadlines, lapses and frays of all sorts, but we're all putting a tremendous effort forward, doing our best, and I'm confident that our community will somehow emanate the warmth, spirit and goodwill that it's taken to create it. (Our vision statement still inspires!)"

Making Some Changes
to Have a Couple of Affordable Units

Gwen's March chart showed that move-ins would be starting in July in the East End; the common house where I would live, would be ready for occupancy in August 1997. The whole project would be complete by October 1997. Carla was negotiating with the Cambridge Housing Authority (CHA) and it looked as though the CHA might buy a unit or two if we could bring the prices down far enough to be within its budget. We decided that the CHA units wouldn't have parking places in the garage and that, with other adjustments, we might make it. We were still working on our by-laws, which would be in our deeds and would be difficult to change, and our rules and regulations which could be more flexible. We searched for more savings and decided to eliminate the trash chute in the common house and the laundry rooms on each floor of the common house, settling for one laundry room in the basement. I reported on a survey about how we would use our common rooms, and Jon produced a detailed report on washing machines and dryers.

In the design committee meetings, which met at Barbara and Ted's house, we continued designing our common house, choosing the color of our siding and trying to stay within our budget. At one impasse, Betsy proposed to authorize one thousand dollars for a consultation with Katherine McCamant, who, with her husband, Chuck Durrett, had written the book that brought cohousing to the United States. We wanted her ideas about the sizes and arrangement of our common areas, especially our living room, which many of us felt was too large and not inviting or cozy enough. Katie affirmed what many of us thought; Bruce made some adjustments.

Meanwhile, Don worked mightily, although without much support, at building a social structure for our growing buildings. In the newsletter, he published mission statements and agreements from other communities, hoping that we would do something along those lines. He also organized a Group Process Training Workshop. Jerry Koch-Gonzalez, from Pioneer Valley Cohousing, came on March 15 to lead it. Just as we had not yet discussed the values that brought us together, we had not drawn up a list of agreements. A new Community Committee was announced in the April newsletter. "As we get closer to moving in, the current crop of pressing decisions about construction will be supplanted by decisions about how we actually want to live together. . . . After we build the buildings, we can build a community." We had, of course, been building our community all along, and all the difficulties and successes we were having in getting together on the construction of the buildings would be the germs of the difficulties and successes we would experience once we moved in.

On the side of the commons, we were getting to know one another. At our general meetings, we usually arranged to have a break with some refreshments, which did give us a chance to chat. Often after a meeting, some of us would go out to a restaurant together. Meetings were open, and the general meetings were well attended.

However, there were also many times when the practices that would give us a commons were overwhelmed by the practices that thwarted our commons. Equality is important in a commons, and from Gwen to the members of the DOC, we were building hierarchies of power and knowledge. The secret arrangements that some of us were making with Bruce were creating privilege and inequalities, winners and losers, and, for the losers, feelings of frustration.

The early-April newsletter broadcast a new complaint from Bruce:

> There is a need for additional patience and civility in this whole process. There have been a number of incidents lately involving our interaction with cohousers that indicate a lack of trust, patience, possibly respect, and certainly civility. Rather than list a number of uncomfortable moments, we would rather ask that you 1) . . . 2) . . . 3) respect the general understanding of the LLP that units were never meant to be customized in every detail.

Of course, he was right: If we were building a commons, we should have been striving for equality; the units should not have been customized in any detail at all.

The April 23 newsletter carried a warning from Bruce that "customizing of units, change orders, and the like, interfere with getting the work done. . . . I encourage all the hard-working task forces to quickly finish the design decisions, so that interior finishes, the landscape, etc. won't hold up your moving in."

In the same newsletter, Carla announced that we were already a beacon. The First Church in Cambridge selected Cambridge Cohousing to be honored at their Social Vision Bazaar. The Reverend Allen Happe said that our community was selected "because [of] your exciting social vision represented by your organization's goals and missions, your organization's importance to the greater Boston Community, your organization's contribution to the celebration of diversity . . . and your grassroots approach to bringing your vision to reality."

By late April, things were looking up again. The landscape committee hired a landscape architect, who came to a meeting where we made long lists of what we hoped we could put on our acre and a quarter that wasn't taken up with buildings, paths, and private patios. There was general agreement that the fences separating us from the street would not be high, and hopes that kids could sled down the hill from our glade to the tracks . . . until someone pointed out that the hill would be about the length of a single sled. Gwen said our boxes would start arriving soon from the factory in New Hampshire and that this was a bit ahead of schedule. The contractor had started building the foundations and she would begin conducting site visits on Mondays.

In May, the first boxes began arriving from New Hampshire. Gwen's time chart still showed the common house move-in as early as August, although possibly as late as the end of October. We were still planning an early-November inaugural celebration. We had completed our bylaws and we set up a committee to draft our rules and regulations, which had to be in place before we could move in. But what took most of our energies during the month of May was the resolution of the thorny question of who would get the last remaining two-bedroom unit in the common house.

When we chose our units in January, there were still six units available, and as we had more than enough singles, we agreed that we would accept no more. However, things got mixed up and we promised our last two-bedroom unit to three households: Two were couples and one was Nancy, a single woman who was planning to adopt a child from China. She hoped that being a member of a cohousing community would improve her chances of getting the child and that, because she planned on having the child, we would consider hers a household with a child and not a single-person household.

At the May 5 meeting, Nancy said that our admission process was costly and confusing and that if she were not given the unit, she would consider the situation outrageous and a serious breach of agreements and faith. We didn't settle the issue at that meeting, but by the next meeting the young couple had dropped out, saying they couldn't afford the unit, the older couple agreed to buy another unit, and Nancy said she thought the situation might be amenable to mediation and that she had never had any plans to sue. She got the unit.

At our May 18 meeting, we decided that we needed to have more fun. Our frivolity facilitator, Ellen, led a discussion of things to do together, especially with kids, which included trips to Walden Pond or the beach, and painting our fences ourselves to save money. As at every meeting, Art reported on our financial situation, our progress with getting everyone's 30 percent down payment, and our application for a building loan from MHIC, the Massachusetts Housing Investment Corporation, which helps to finance affordable housing and community building. We then turned to planning our life after move-in. Barbara asked us to imagine what it would be like to come home starving next March and have food on the table. The rules and regulations task force led a meeting that included suggested rules about pets in the common house, parking spaces and whether they could be rented or sold, guest rooms, smoking in common spaces, and TV in common areas.

On June 1, Gwen handed out a revised move-in schedule. She explained that due to delays of unit deliveries from Epoch, the East End would not be ready for move-in until September and the other areas would not be available until early November. However, she added that Carl tended to be pessimistic and the dates might move up. Karen, who had two school-age children, pointed out that the move-in dates were crucial for those who had kids in school and needed to know which school they would be attending in the fall. There was also the problem that banks would give only a sixty-day mortgage guarantee. Gwen said she would announce updates as often as she could.

We were still waiting for our loan from MHIC. It had many conditions, one being that we would have at least three affordable units. Carla was working with the Cambridge Housing Authority to get them, but there were problems: HUD (the U. S. Department of Housing and Urban Development) would fund only two- and three-bedroom units, and the one person who was a member and could qualify for subsidized housing was interested in a studio; our prices were way over what CHA usually paid (sixty thousand dollars for a two-bedroom unit), and if CHA did purchase a unit, it couldn't guarantee that the resident we would prefer would get it.

Joan, whom I'd met at our first meeting and who headed up the membership committee, announced that our membership now included fifteen singles, thirteen families with children, and ten households of two or more adults, all adding up to sixty-one adults, twenty of them over the age of fifty, nineteen children under the age of fifteen, and four older teens, for a total of eighty-four people. We still had two units to fill: a large town house for $290,000 and a four-bedroom flat with two bathrooms in the common house for $270,000. Joan said she didn't want to have to deal with the diversity issue anymore. She didn't like having to tell people that if they were white, they could be bumped by somebody who was Black. Still, the group had to deal with the question of how to keep the diversity we had and add to it. We decided to have a Friends of Cohousing category for people who couldn't move in with us but who could participate so that we would get to know them and they would be sure that cohousing was what they really wanted.

By late June, Gwen had set the first move-in date back to October and, in July, her charts showed that common house move-ins might be as early as October or as late as the end of November. Our inaugural celebration was rescheduled for around Thanksgiving. The good news was that we were sold out.

Seven

Private Gardens and the Commons

Spring 1997

Spring 1997 brought the need to grapple with an issue that put the difference between our private property and our commons into stark relief. We had to decide how much of the land abutting our town houses and first-floor units would belong to those units and how much of that land would be part of our commons. The arguments each side mustered in defense of private property or the commons, although never articulated in exactly those terms, highlight our cultural values along the axes of variation between the market and the commons and between private property at one end and the common wealth at the other.

The issue first came up at a meeting that I didn't hear about until almost a decade later. I was having a dinner on our patio that Francesca had arranged for a few founders and two couples who had just moved in. The conversation turned to this book. One of the men, also a sociologist, asked what it would be about. I said it was about Cambridge Cohousing and that I would be focusing on how, as we planned our community, boundaries shifted between our commons and our private property. For example, I said, one of our earliest battles had been over private gardens. Hearing that,

Francesca hid her face in her napkin and said, "Oh no, I don't want to go there. That was the worst meeting ever."

"What meeting?" I asked.

"It was at the developer's office and it got so bad, people went storming out."

Viv said she didn't remember that meeting. I didn't, either, but I did remember a bunch of meetings about gardens. The sociologist wanted to know what private gardens were.

Viv explained, pointing to the fences that hid the gardens alongside Tim and Lyn's and Art and Gwen's units and to Bert and Isabel's unfenced garden. When we chose our units on January 5, 1997, we weren't thinking about fences and private gardens. We knew where our units would be, how many bedrooms, baths, and windows we would have, and roughly what our units would cost, but we did not know exactly where the lines would be drawn, especially the lines between the outdoor space attached to the first-floor units and town houses and our common outdoor spaces. The first time those lines were marked on paper and remarked upon at a meeting was the one Francesca remembered so painfully and Viv and I knew nothing about.

I did remember a phone call, which I think was from Joan. "How do you feel about private gardens?" she'd asked. Still living in Connecticut, going up to Cambridge for meetings whenever I could, I had no idea what she was talking about. I said I had no feelings or thoughts about private gardens. Gwen's description of sylvan paths through flowering orchards and Frisbee frolicking on our great lawn still danced in my head. But by the end of the call, I agreed that private gardens wouldn't be a good idea.

Like most of our ideas, our idea of gardens depended on how and where we had been raised. I was born in New Jersey and lived there until I was six, when we moved to New York City. I had dim memories of our backyard in New Jersey, but until Dick and I were no longer living in the city, I could not imagine what it would be

like to have a private garden. An aunt had a small patch of dirt behind her garden apartment in Greenwich Village. I loved that scrap
of private outdoor space and wished I could have something like
it. I and everybody else I knew lived in an apartment, and in those
days in New York City, and perhaps in most cities, balconies were
almost as uncommon as gardens. The closest we came to a garden
were the flowers that florists wrapped in green waxy paper, and the
closest I ever got to a private garden was something my brother and
I would give our mother on Mother's Day. We'd go to Woolworth's.
There we would pick out a "garden." In a ceramic pot about three
inches wide by six inches long and about four inches deep were
two or three little plants, a rock or two, and maybe even a ceramic
dog, child, or bench. Each year, as Mother's Day approached, we
would look for last year's "garden." Not finding it (probably because
it would have dried out by then), we knew just what to give our
mother for the coming Mother's Day.

Cohousers, as they invent new divisions between the public
and the private, spend a lot of time drawing visible and invisible
boundaries to determine where their private property meets their
commons, or, in Sahlin's terms, where they intend to reciprocate
and where they intend to pool. To put it in yet another way, we had
to decide exactly where what would be mine or yours would meet
what would be ours. Cohousing communities carve out more common space than is usual in contemporary Western neighborhoods,
and they soften the boundaries between private and communal
space to encourage more shared activities, more socializing, and to
create an environment that will dispel the loneliness so emblematic
of our contemporary world. Sometimes our attempts to create more
warmth can generate heat.

Sometime after Francesca's dinner, I was picking veggies from
our common garden right beside David and Joan's patio, when
David invited me over for a glass of wine. Taking advantage of this
opportunity to find out about the meeting I'd missed, I asked Joan

if she could remember the phone call she made in the spring of '97. She couldn't. When I told her more about the call, it became clear that either my memory and notes were failing me and she was not the person who'd called me or that her position had completely changed. Not only couldn't she remember ever having been against private gardens; she now defended them: "You certainly wouldn't want people walking right past your living room slider, would you?" I silently noted that her patio separated our common vegetable garden from her living room sliders.

David remembered the meeting. He said that it was Peter who'd noticed on the plans Gwen presented that a large garden with a high fence surrounding it would be part of her unit. "It would have been a fortress," David said. Joan objected to the word *fortress,* but David insisted in a voice that had a slight squeak, making it clear he was sticking to *fortress.* I didn't want to get bogged down there, so I asked what had happened. He said that after many meetings, the DOC had decided to bring the issue to a general meeting.

When we are preparing to make an important decision, we sometimes go through an exercise called "hopes and fears." At the front of the room, there will be one or two newsprint pads on easels, each with a scribe standing by with a Magic Marker to write down comments as we go around the room saying what we think about the issue at hand. The first to speak at the meeting where we did a "hopes and fears" about gardens and fences was Fran, a rotund singer and pianist about forty years old, who thought interior fences should be high enough so that kids' games and other activities wouldn't bother people—for example, that their balls wouldn't roll into private spaces and their hide-and-seek games wouldn't spill into private gardens. Peter followed, saying that he hoped there would be low fences or no fences between private areas and common areas, but he thought that it would be okay to have fences at the outside borders of our site. When it came to his turn, David agreed, adding that he hoped there would be no barriers within the community and that we'd have public areas all over the property with benches to sit on and paths so we could walk through the whole community. David echoed Peter, saying that he hoped that when you wanted to be private, you'd have to go into your house. When we got to Beverly, who would soon be living in a town house and who was almost the last to speak, she repeated what was becoming the more general hope that there would be no fences within the site, and that we'd all feel welcomed into all edges and quarters of our property. On related matters, Betsy said she was worried that our common garden and shared spaces would be eaten away by big private spaces. Someone else hoped that we could get a complete plan of the outside space, showing how the public and private areas would be divided. Olga, a tall retired science teacher, who would be our conscience on sustainability matters, said we should look at Harvard's Linnaean Street student housing, which had dark asphalt walks and private spaces separated by ivy, with the whole surrounded by a brick wall. "It gives a feeling of privacy and yet is open," she said. Someone else said she hoped we'd check with other cohousing communities to see how they separated public and private spaces. Then someone hoped that no one would say "You can't come through my yard" to kids. Peter said he hoped there would be outdoor space to store gardening equipment and kids' outdoor toys. Finally, Gwen warned that we should pay attention to the recommendations of the landscape architect and to the maintenance of gardens and their cost.

By then, it was about 5:00 P.M. and we had run out of time. Charles, a bearded teacher and Becky's husband, who was facilitating the discussion, concluded by hoping that the Landscape committee would set it all up to meet everybody's needs. Peter said that the Landscape committee was overwhelmed and invited others to help resolve these issues. So Charles invited everybody to get involved. Fran volunteered to lead the group, and seven others joined. After a break, Fran announced that the new public/private task force would meet the next day at the Design committee meeting.

The next day, Charles sent an email with the subject heading "Public space, landscape issues and West End stairs": "Just so we're clear, this is being talked about a bit at landscape and design meetings, but now will be under the aegis of the new task force Fran is convening."

To which Fran responded, "My understanding is that we will discuss the outdoor space issues tonight at Design, and if that committee feels it is necessary, we will spin it off to the task force who volunteered yesterday."

The next day, Charles asked, "So what happened?" And Fran replied, "A lot happened. . . . We clarified the goals of the task force: 1) delineating public and private spaces, and 2) developing guidelines for use of private spaces." A few days later, Fran sent out an invitation to another meeting:

> The task force with the longest name will meet Monday, August 25 at 7 p.m. at Barbara and Ted's. I have been gathering information and opinion on this issue, and welcome phone calls and emails from anyone in the community. It seems to me the issue breaks down into three major parts: 1. Do private gardens or yards exist? Some people dispute this, though our Mission Statement does say in regard to outdoor space ". . . and some private gardens." 2. If they exist, where are the boundaries? Many people are concerned about inequity in the size of such areas, or their locations impeding flow to and from public space. 3. How can owners use/delineate private spaces? Are fences allowed, if so how high? etc. Please chime in, and come to the meeting if you are interested. I am hopeful that we can settle our differences over this in a constructive, positive way. The potential for acrimony is there, and unfortunately some of the discussion has already felt personal. I hope I am the right person to help work this out,

and since my unit clearly has no outdoor space perhaps I can be somewhat neutral. Let's work together and figure this out.

Though she worked hard to appear neutral and probably thought she was being so, Fran's introduction to the next meeting clearly favored private property over the commons. She emphasized the rights and privileges of property while giving only a slight nod to what it might take to build a common:

> We are pioneers in urban cohousing development, guidelines are not available. We approach this process acknowledging that we have chosen our units (a major life decision, indeed) based on both the estimated price of those units and what we believe we are getting for that price. Any changes that affect those expectations must be taken very seriously, considering the impact on individuals involved as well as the community as a whole. . . . We have to base decisions on a "social economy" model of cohousing. On the one hand, we place a high value on, and therefore hope to encourage, casual interaction among community members. This translates into a desire for as much public outdoor space as possible on our site. On the other hand, we will balance this desire for community interaction against each person's privacy, pride and enjoyment of his or her own home. To achieve this balance, it may be helpful to do a kind of "cost/benefit analysis." Does a particular area's value to the community as public space (considering its potential usefulness, cost and maintenance as a public area) outweigh its value as private space to the abutting individual unit owner(s)?
>
>   Notes: Some outdoor space may have an amplified impact on a particular unit's indoor space, depending on how the two are connected. For example, a patio outside a sliding glass door continues the feeling of private indoor space outdoors, and relieves the inhabitants from feeling uncomfortably exposed. (Without a

transitional area from inside to outside, curious children, dogs and voyeurs could press their wet noses directly against one's door and peer into one's living space. Even though these events are unlikely to happen, it is the psychological perception that they might that causes discomfort.) An example of this type of private space is the patio area outside unit 115, facing the glade. Other areas are not so clear in their value as public or private spaces.

At about this time, Florence tried to clarify some legal points and, in the process, made a stab at stating the claims of the commons:

Given the very limited open space on the site it seems to me inconceivable that the group as a whole would agree that such a substantial area should become "privatized." The same is true for all but a patio-sized area in the "glade." It seems quite contrary to the whole idea of community ownership of common space to carve out such substantial private spaces and fence them off from use by the majority of community members.

Peter concurred, sounding a bit like the "Law of the Sea," by which nations establish their rights to protect the resources of the sea out to a certain distance from their coast:

The idea of "private" outdoor property in a community like ours is a contradiction in terms, and one to which I do not subscribe. Do ground floor dwellers "own" the ground space adjacent to their units, or simply have "prior right," however you call it? And to what extent do they "own" that land area—out to the spine line, or to the edge of the property line, or to the nearest sidewalk, internal or external to the property? How far down? How far up? I do not offer these questions as challenges for the sake of argument, nor to provoke you. I do think that our Co-Housing concept is not yet perfect—it is still developing, and some of the questions with which we have dealt and are dealing are visible

evidence of that imperfect vision. This matter of private property
within the common property is one of them.

There were other issues beyond just how much land would be attached to the town houses and the ground-floor flats. One was the
question of promises. As a developer, Gwen was concerned that we
would be able to turn over every unit to private hands the minute it
was ready. Any delay would raise the cost of the units for everybody. In this effort, some of us thought that she might have made
the kinds of promises that developers often make: promises that
might not be kept, that cannot be forced by contract, and that probably don't matter much in the short-lived world of markets and
exchange.

In the long-term world of commons and cooperation, however,
promises and mistakes made in 1997 would haunt us for as long as
we would be living together as a community. When Fran referred
to our choice of units and what we thought we were getting for
the price of our units, she was thinking in market terms. So was
Florence, who was a lawyer, when she addressed those expectations
and promises in her email:

> The group as a whole never did take up the question of pri-
> vate areas and no plans that I ever saw specifically showed private
> yards. There was always an agreement that as many units as
> possible should have a private outdoor sitting area. It was my
> understanding that this meant: for most of the flats, a 4 x 12
> balcony; for ground-floor flats and town houses, a 10 x 12 patio.
> . . . It is true that there are a number of plans which have dark
> green lines drawn here and there which some people apparently
> thought indicated private yards. But since the plans do vary and
> some of the green lines clearly do NOT indicate yards, this doesn't
> mean much. I thought they indicated landscaping such as shrubs!
> I suspect that Gwen may have sold some of the town houses with

the promise that they would come with a private garden. However, in my opinion she had no right to do so, and the group has
no obligation to make good on her word in this instance. At this
time, no one has a legal right to use any area. The Master Deed,
which we have yet to review as a group, will identify "Exclusive
Use Areas" by reference to a Site Plan.

In addition to the large area by Gwen and Art's town house (across
the path from Peter's town house), the second zone of major
contention was the west end of the "spine." Originally, Gwen designed the spine as a hard-surface path that would run from a driveway at the east end of our property to a pocket park and stairway
to the garage at the west end.

We held another session of hopes and fears about the west end
pocket park and its stairway. Gwen, who now wanted to cut off the
spine before her unit and the west end town houses, argued that
if we kept the stairs, there would be more ways for outsiders to get
in and there would be less security because you could not see this
entrance from the common house. Others argued that without an
opening at the west end there would be no reason for anyone to
go into the west end cul-de-sac; it would become a private enclave,
contradicting our mission statement of openness. Others imagined
an open spine: Joan said she wanted to be able to take a nice stroll
and have a place to sit and hang out when doddering out at age
eighty. Florence pointed out that community happens when people
hang out on their stoops: Passersby may stop to chat; a beverage
may be brought out. "You need a place to park yourself and wait
for folks to come by," she said. Meryl said she wanted to go with
her newspaper "to await others on a bench, not a big lawn, just a
piece of garden for those without one to lure others from opposite
ends of the property."

When all was said and the plans were done, we ended up with
three types of outdoor space: first, public areas that would be open

to the entire community; second, areas outside individual units that would go with specific units and be for the exclusive use of the owners of that unit; third, areas that were not clearly either public or exclusive-use areas. These areas were deeded to the specific units, and the owners agreed (1) that there would be no fences or hedges placed around these areas; (2) that these areas would be kept green; and (3) that they would be visually and physically accessible to the community. The garden on the north side of Gwen and Art's unit was of this sort. Sometimes, over the years, Peter would put up a hammock and demonstratively enjoy the space, perhaps making sure that community use, or at least his use, of that part of our little acre and a quarter would be preserved by his squatting on it.

The stairs to the garage never did come back into our plans, and the pocket garden with benches that was supposed to bring people to the west end of our property never materialized, so that, over time, the design of our common outdoor spaces tended to encourage neighborhood cliques. The west end, cut off as it was at the path to the street in front of Art and Gwen's, encouraged a group of mostly young families to socialize almost exclusively in the west end cul-de-sac; the east end, partly because the residents there would move in about a half year before the rest and partly because they were separated from the rest of the community by the long glade, became another neighborhood; and those living in the common house became a third group, although a less cohesive one.

A central cohousing design principle is to provide as many opportunities as possible for contact among residents. McCamant and Durrett have much to say about the social benefits of a "soft edge" between the front of a private dwelling and the common areas— semiprivate areas, such as front porches or patios where residents can set out tables and chairs or plant a small garden. This space provides an easily accessible spot where people can sit and watch or invite neighbors to share an iced tea on a summer evening. That must have been what Peter, David, and Meryl had in mind when they said they didn't want any interior fencing and they thought that there should be community spaces for strolling, sitting, and chatting in all parts of the property.

A very few units—David and Joan's, Harriet and Paul's, Lyn and Jim's, Art and Gwen's, Isabel and Bert's, and Rosie's—have patios big enough for a table and chairs, but only David and Joan and Lyn and Jim use their patios that way. The town houses along the path have room for a grill and table and chairs, and their owners sometimes use their space, but David and Joan are the only ones who often invite other cohousers to their patio for a meal or a glass of wine. The rest of the private outdoor spaces hardly ever became sites of casual socializing.

These areas are exposed, but they also have a private feeling, and you wouldn't even talk to someone on their private patio unless they talked to you first, thus inviting you to cross the invisible boundary. I was reminded of that the other day when I went to our vegetable garden to pick some greens. Jon and Lori, their son, and some friends were having dinner on their patio. They were engrossed in their conversation and I didn't know whether to say hi or not, so I waited for them to initiate a greeting. When they didn't, I went about my picking as quickly as I could, feeling quite awkward and wondering whether they did, too. Then I slipped away as invisibly as I could.

The feeling is quite different in front of the common house. Our not-so-great lawn and the path by it works as the kind of commons that nurtures community. Children play on the jungle gym or run around the yard while their parents watch and chat. Here you wouldn't pass someone without a greeting. The area gives the kind of feeling that Florence imagined as a place to park yourself and wait for folks to come by and chat.

Eight

Moving Out and Moving In—
My Year Without a Home

While we were imagining what life would be like with or without private gardens, many of us were beginning a year without a garden, a fence, or even a roof over our heads. On our way to a community where we hoped to enjoy the warmth of many nearby friends, we were out in the cold. We had begun our year of rooflessness. Again and again, Gwen had said, "What I am worried about is whether people will be ready to close on time." It was a typical developer's concern, but not one that considered our special situation, where all but those who were granted exemptions had already put down a 30 percent deposit and six of us had bankrolled our land purchase. Nevertheless, in response to Gwen's exhortations, several of us had sold our homes and were renting high-priced interim housing; others were relying on the hospitality of friends.

My vagabondage began in June 1997. In April, I had called Gwen to find out when our units would be ready. "June," she'd said. Noting that none of the prefabricated units had been delivered by Epoch, the company in New Hampshire that was building them, I asked, "Are you sure?" "Well, maybe not until late June," she responded. I put my New Haven house on the market. The April newsletter noted that four others had already accepted offers or signed Purchase and Sale agreements.

In May, when I got an offer for my house, Gwen's chart showed completion in June even though only a few of the units had been delivered from New Hampshire. I called Gwen again to ask when she thought the project would be complete. "Your unit will be ready in June," she said. I signed a Purchase and Sale agreement with a woman who wanted to close in June.

A few days later, the May newsletter arrived and I knew I was in trouble. Gwen's chart now showed move-ins beginning in mid-September and finishing by the end of October. Barbara and Ted invited me to stay in their house for the duration. But, as my closing neared, they offered their room to Francesca and Gerard, who had already sold their home. Barbara asked friends who summered on Nantucket if they'd like a house sitter. They said they would, but they wouldn't be leaving Cambridge until July 4. In June, my friend Linda took me in. Linda's house is down a driveway, behind the ART theater, in Cambridge. Couldn't be a better location or a more beautiful house. Unfortunately, relations between Linda and me soured when she tired of taking messages that friends and family left for me on her phone. Writing this in 2021, it's hard to remember a world without cell phones. They had been invented by 1997, but they were large clunky boxes meant for cars, not the slim ubiquitous instruments we now slip into our pockets.

Being without a landline or a permanent address would be among the worst aspects of my year of rooflessness. To make matters even worse, in order to have time to start a new research project and promote my book, which would come out that year, I started a sabbatical leave in June and therefore was not even going to my office, where I might have received mail and phone calls.

Fortunately, I did not have to annoy Linda for long. On July 5, I moved into the best house I have ever lived in. Huge, beautiful, on historic Brattle Street, it shared a backyard fence with the president of Harvard. However, when summer ended, so did delivery of our prefab units from Epoch. The company claimed to be on the verge of bankruptcy. Construction came to a halt. Gwen and Art said they were sorry the modules weren't coming in on time, and they asked Carl, our contractor, to give Epoch an advance so production would start up again. He did and it did.

About then, Gwen's charts began to show a new feature: not just dots, shaded lines, and slash marks but arrows, too. The dots of April showed the original plan for project completion; the shaded areas, added in May, showed a hoped-for completion; the slash marks, added in July, showed a likely completion by Thanksgiving; and new arrows reaching out to the end of December showed the new possible completion time. Common house move-ins, we were told, might be delayed till then. Somehow, I would have to find shelter for the rest of the year.

At our August general meeting, when Gwen displayed the new chart with the arrows, she said that the project would be totally complete and we would all be moved in by the end of November, at the very latest. She blamed the delays on the rest of us, claiming

Cambridge Cohousing Projected Schedule Through Move-in (Rev 8/19/97)*										
Threshold Dates	May	Jun	Jul	Aug	Sep	Oct	Nov			
West End buyers finalize choices										
Sign GMP										
Foundations/modules-East End	• •	✔								
Delivery of modules-East End		• •	✔							
Foundations Common Hs/West End		• • • • • •	✔							
East End/Button-up			• • • • • • • •	///////// ±						
Deliver modules Common Hs			• • • • ?							
Drill geothermal wells (West End)			?	/////						
Common Hs Button-up			• • • •						
Utilities hook-up for East End			• • • •						
C.O.East End units/move in			? • •	/////////// ?					
West stacked flats/twnhses delivered			• • • •	///////////					
West stacked flats/twnhses button-up			• • • •	/////////					
101, 102, 103 modules delivered**			• •	///// ?					
Bsmt button-up/utilities for C.Hs/West End			• • • •						
C Hs, West End, stacked flats C.O./move in			• • •	⟶					
Utilities, site work complete			• • • • • • • •	⟶					
Thanksgiving/Celebration				•	end of Dec?				

notes: • = 4/97 schedule; ▬ = 6/97 schedule; ///// = 8/97 schedule. C.O.=certificate of occupancy
*The Epoch crew is working as hard as it possibly can, and Carl is doing his best to handle delays and changes—Gwen
**All West End & C.Hs units depend on delivery of 101, 102, 103 for utility hook-up because site entry of water & electricity is in their bsmts. If this delivery schedule moves, so do move-in dates.

that she at first planned to have construction starting in December 1996 but that many decisions had not been made at that time and we couldn't get our order to Epoch before the company began work on its summer obligations. Also, the company had been short-handed during the spring and summer. Carl, she said, was pushing to move the work along. She said that he was a very competent contractor and was doing his best to keep up with our schedule. His contract would end at the end of November. She concluded by saying that the developers could do nothing for those suffering from the late move-ins except to feel bad.

On August 24, I facilitated another general meeting. (By that time, everybody but me seemed to have forgotten the disastrous meeting of two summers ago, and I was occasionally asked to facilitate general meetings.) At this one, Bert, one of our two psychiatrists, introduced an exercise to help calm the atmosphere by bringing concerns into the open. "Most of us are inexperienced at cohousing and at buying a home, and feelings sometimes run high," he said. "It's hard to get time lines decided, and frustrations may boil over on a small matter." He then assigned each of us to one of six small groups, where we discussed our feelings about the project. A few minutes later, we gathered again in the big room, and a presenter from each group reported on the issues raised in their group.

Most problems were about how we were communicating and governing ourselves. Members said they were unhappy with rumors and were concerned with how decisions were being made. They were frustrated by being on a task force when decisions the task force was supposed to make had already been made. Someone pointed out the difficulty of following a slow consensus process and at the same time meeting demands for the quick decisions necessary for construction. It wasn't clear to many when and how amateurs could participate in professional discussions. It was hard, said another, to be part of the decision making because of inconvenient committee meeting times. Email etiquette was a problem for others.

A sense of inequality was felt by a member who complained that squeaky and powerful wheels got the grease.

Divisions were forming. Although we did not have the racial or ethnic diversity we had hoped for, income and stage of life differences were generating difficulties. Money was a problem. Some worried about whether they would have enough to meet the obligations they had made, especially in the face of "groundless optimism that underestimated the cost of the project and raised the threat of having to pay more down the road." Interest rates were going up, and the recalculations of the pricing task force worried some. Many found it difficult to talk about money problems with speakers of different financial capabilities. My biggest complaint was that I had no home and my spectacular summer house-sitting arrangement was about to end. Several others complained about their rooflessness or about their fears of becoming roofless. "The moving-in dates keep moving and the time line is behind the eight ball," complained one of my fellow vagabonds.

It wasn't all complaints, though. Some members said they appreciated the beauty of our buildings, they were pleased by our process of decision making, and they felt we were getting good financial information from the DOC and the developers. They were especially impressed that the final budget was so close to the original.

I scrounged around, looking for a rental for the fall, and finally found a cute little place for a high rent in Cambridgeport, a section of Cambridge midway between our site in North Cambridge and Boston. The space and furnishings were good, but the place was filthy. Under the grime, you could tell it had good bones. The owner promised to clean it up, and I signed a lease for September through November.

A few weeks after I moved in, I invited a bunch of cohousers to dinner. David asked how I could stand living in such a dirty place. I said the owner had promised to clean it and I'd even paid to have a cleaning service spend a day working on it, but it was hopeless.

The owner had a couple of cats and a dog; there was no way to get the floors clean, short of sanding.

At Gwen's construction update at the September 7, 1997, meeting, she said she had just come from the site, and it looked ready for steel, a major milestone on the way to completion. The rest of the common house and West End would get built quickly now, she promised. The wells for the heat pump had been dug. One of three cranes that would set our boxes in place would be coming the next day and staying until all the units were in. Heating, she said, was critical for move-in, and the East End could be ready for move-in by November. For our part, we must finish our pricing, the bylaws, the master deed, and the final plans, especially the landscape plan. Fannie Mae approval, condo fees, and miscellaneous documents all had to be in place before we could take possession of our units. Gwen warned that the next couple of weeks would be frantic.

At that meeting we chose our first nine-member managing board. I was pleased to be the fifth person and the second woman to be chosen. At our first meeting, I became the vice chairperson and the liaison to the DOC.

I facilitated the September 28, 1997, general meeting at the BB&N Middle School where Isabel, who had worked there, had arranged a room and the custodian's services for us. We had to be out by 6:30. Once again, I was having a hard time moving the meeting along and making sure that everyone got a chance to speak. When Deb interrupted a speaker, I stopped her, assuring her that she'd get her turn. She stormed out. Her husband, Jeff, said she was like that, not to worry. I worried; I'm like that.

In October, I began to wheeze. Though I had never before had allergies, breathing was becoming difficult. The days were getting colder and I was getting sicker. I called the mover to ask if I could get some winter clothes out of storage. He said that my stuff in the storage facility was all shrink-wrapped and if I broke into the wrapping, he couldn't be responsible for what might happen to my things. I never again saw the set of Waterford crystal we had inherited from Dick's mother or my favorite KLH radio.

At a meeting in November, Art and Gwen again said they were sorry the prefabricator wasn't delivering the modules on time. Gwen's chart now showed a January move-in. One of the biggest problems, she said, was getting the whole heating system working. The woman I was renting from said I could stay until January 1 but not a day longer. The word was that Carl, the builder, had to finish by January 1 because our contract with him had a penalty clause and it would cost him for every day after January 1 that the buildings weren't finished. However, when January rolled around, the buildings still weren't ready. My friend Carol said I could stay at her place until my unit was ready. It turned out that Carl could wiggle out of the penalty clause.

On New Year's Day, 1998, I moved to Carol's house. She lived in a lovely house only a couple of blocks from Linda's, but the room she had for me was just large enough to squeeze in a twin bed and a desk. By this time, I had taken my winter clothes and my cross-country skis out of storage and there was no room for everything, even though I tightly stuffed things into the space under the bed. Gwen's chart now showed a March common house move-in date. Those with units in the East End, she said, would be able to move in by January. Paul and Harriet, who would be moving into a town house in the East End said I could live in their house until it was sold or my unit was ready, whichever came first.

At a meeting on Saturday, January 3, at Harriet and Paul's, Harriet showed me around. I was excited that if the East End really did close on January 22, as promised, I would be able to leave my cubicle at Carol's house and live in Harriet and Paul's large, comfortable home until mine was ready. I felt that they were being enormously generous. Right about then, an officer from East Cambridge Savings

Bank, where I had applied for a mortgage, called to answer some questions I had sent him. He seemed impressed with our group. "They're all such nice people," he said.

On Sunday, January 18, at the general meeting, Gwen said that when she predicted early move-in dates, she was being optimistic, and that because she'd predicted wrong, people got upset with her and so now she would not predict anymore; she would not even give out a range of move-in dates.

Francesca said to me, "She just doesn't get it. As long as she's not the one without a home." Around that time, I began having imaginary conversations with Gwen. The problem with predicting wrong, I wanted to tell her, is not that people get upset with you, but that people are damaged in ways that you refuse to acknowledge: They lose things, they can't sleep, and they jeopardize their mental and physical health. I wish last year at this time you had said we might move in as early as June 1997 but as late as June 1998. I and others might not have sold the houses we were living in or I might have found a sublet for a year and moved two times instead of six.

Lending her weight to the market side of our axis of variation, Gwen often criticized us and praised Carl. She seemed to divide us into friends who favored market values and foes who favored values associated with the commons. The good guys were the pros; commoners were the enemy, who had to be kept in line. As we approached the day when the East Enders would be signing off on their units and moving in, Gwen said that her worries came from her professional experience: On other jobs, people wouldn't sign off because of the smallest blemish.

As I was getting ready to move into her place, Harriet and I got to talking about how late the project was. Referring to Gwen and Art, I said, "They used to say that it was because we hadn't gotten going with Epoch last winter, but now they are saying that it is because we've allowed too much customization." That really got to Harriet. "Well, I'd like Gwen to say that to me," she said, "because

I'd tell her that the one with all the customization was her. Do you remember when we all went up to Epoch and we were going to lunch and Gwen couldn't come to lunch with us because she asked to speak to the designer at Epoch about her kitchen? The rest of us weren't able to custom-design our kitchens."

When Harriet noted that none of the rest of us could do something that Gwen had done, she had put her finger on a central feature of a commons: equality. Every special privilege that Gwen took for herself or gave to a friend or loud complainer stabbed at the heart of our fledgling commons. She was only doing what developers always do and she had been doing for so long that it must have seemed like second nature to her. But every time that she or others in leadership positions took something special for themselves or gave something special to a friend, they were acting like competitors in a marketplace, rather than like commoners in a community. The blemishes, some visible in our physical structures and others harder to see in our feelings and relationships, would live on in the little world we were creating, making it a less perfect union. Yes, in a commons, you can give special assistance to someone who may be falling below the level of the group, but, no, you cannot appropriate a part of the group's wealth to create inequality within the group—at least not if you are trying to build a strong commons. *Commoning* (used as a verb, as Lewis Hyde suggests) brings a group of commoners toward equality and a level playing field, while exchanges in a market tend to increase difference and inequality among players.

On Wednesday, January 21, I registered my car at my new address and got my parking sticker so that I could use any Cambridge parking spot. Then I went to the DOC meeting at Gwen and Art's office. Only Stella was there. She didn't know why no one else had showed up for the meeting. I called Ted, thinking he would probably know because Barbara was on the DOC. He said the meeting had been moved to the site. I never did get to that meeting, but, at the next one, I reminded Gwen that I was the liaison between the managing board and the DOC and that when she changed the location of the meeting, she should let me know. "Well, you don't have a fax machine," she explained. "I don't have a home where I could put a fax machine," I reminded her, and suggested that she use email to communicate with me.

At the end of January, the East Enders were finally preparing to move in. Our Listserv was flooded by emails with a new vocabulary, preparing us for our new roles as home owners. One from Bruce, our architect, appeared on Wednesday, January 28:

> By issuing a Substantial Completion Certificate to the builder, with attached punch lists (work still not completed, but noted) the builder can hand over to the LLP (owner), the use of the building. . . . [A]t that point the owner can do what it chooses with the building . . . [people can] move their chattel into their units before they have a Certificate of Occupancy and could actually move themselves in. [On Friday I will] issue the Substantial Completion to the builder for the East End Units as a block. In my opinion, with the punch lists attached, the units are ready for use i.e., they are substantially complete. This does not in any way relieve the builder from completing the work as defined in the contract.

At that point, Florence promised a "Use and Occupancy Agreement so that people would start paying rent to the LLP if they do not close by a specified date." Although some of us, who had been homeless for half a year or more, were champing at the bit, others, just as Gwen feared, were still trying to sell their former homes.

Working with several banks to get the mortgages most of us needed to buy our units, we learned a whole other vocabulary: "prepayment and its terms"; "closing costs"; "title insurance"; and "condominium documents," which needed to be recorded so the banks would have "book and page numbers" so they could issue mortgages. We were advised to get a "declaration of homestead," which would cost seventy dollars and would protect $100,000 of equity in our homes. When Jon tried to explain the difference between a "disclosure statement," which lets you know what charges you would be expected to pay at the closing, and a "commitment letter," which commits the bank to giving you a mortgage, he added, "My bank's idea of commitment is sort of like 'I promise to love you forever as long as you bring me the moon by next Thursday.'" And Josh, who signed his emails with the motto "Worry is a misuse of the imagination," asked, "[Will] the photo ID requested by the lender's attorney delay the closing if my picture is not suitably attractive?"

On January 28, Lulu, who with her husband and toddler daughter were the only ones other than me moving from another state, wrote a long email that described all the papers that needed to be signed before the East Enders could get their keys and move into their units. She concluded on a happy note: "More detailed update and handouts on Sunday. Hang in there—it's looking pretty good!!"

But then on Friday, Karen sent an email with the subject line "Tim and Lulu can't move in!!"

> Since there is no CO yet, Tim and Lulu and Megan are homeless as of Saturday. I tried to find a place for them to stay with a friend of mine. Does anyone know anyone who might be able to host them for a week? Tim and Lulu are going to have to go to a motel if they can't find any place to stay. . . . They won't stay in a home where there are pets, however. If they do have to stay in the motel, I think now would be a really excellent time to invite them over for dinner. And if you are going to have your house vacant during the day because you are working, and it is more or less baby-proof and pet free, perhaps you could invite Lulu and Megan to housesit for you one day so they aren't cooped up in one room.

I wondered why Karen thought the Tim and Lulu' days of wandering were so special; maybe it was because they had a child.

The others who were roofless were all singles or couples without children. They suffered in silence, solving their housing problems privately and individually. Barbara and Ted did step in to offer Francesca and Gerard a room, and I would soon be moving to Harriet and Paul's newly vacated house, but to my knowledge, no one else who still had a home had offered our roofless a place to stay. Nor did our homeless members look to the group for help. The problem may have been group-inflicted, but whatever solutions we might find would be individual. It was one of several signs that we had not yet coalesced into a community. An intentional commons, unlike natural commons, such as the air we breathe, usually develops from a common identity, a shared affinity or challenge, and most of us were not roofless. Percentagewise, Cambridge Cohousing's construction delays, coupled with Gwen's goading us to sell our homes, had probably caused in our small community as much homelessness as a major hurricane, forest fire, or tsunami would cause in a large community, but we were not thinking enough like commoners to consider developing our own little FEMA (Federal Emergency Management Agency). On our axis of variation from commons to market, most of us were still thinking, living, and having expectations mostly at the market pole.

The help offered some of us—for example, Barbara's offer of a room to Francesca, and Gerard and Harriet's offer of her house to me—were all private acts of generosity. They were not a support we had built together to be used when necessary. Once again, we come to the difference between markets and commons. Charity and generosity are gifts that emphasize the difference between givers and receivers. The giver feels good and the receiver feels grateful. On the other hand, taking what you need from a commons increases your sense of belonging to the larger whole. The pool that belongs to all the commoners provides what is needed: Everyone contributes; everyone takes what they need. To take more would be absurd; to contribute less would be freeloading.

On Sunday, February 1, there was a general meeting where Barbara handed out the punch list procedure. Everybody listened carefully to her assurances that, just as Bruce said in his email, we would all be able to visit our units and go over with him everything that seemed broken or unfinished and he would put it on the punch list; then Carl would have to fix any problem within a month.

That sounded okay, but then came the DOC meeting on Tuesday. It was a doozy. David and I had taken our seats around the table, when Art, Barbara, Bruce, and Gwen came in after their site meeting with Carl. Carl was a man who could intimidate almost anyone, and they were visibly shaken.

After settling a bit of preliminary business, we got down to the punch lists. Bruce, the architect, the one who would ordinarily represent the owners, complained: "As quickly as we get things accomplished, new items appear. The process has to be corralled. At this point Carl is throwing up his hands and saying 'I won't have any more of it.' From here on it is warrantee issues, and the managing company has to take it over. I've done my punch lists; now it is up to the managing company."

As the liaison from the managing board, I didn't like the sound of that, because it meant that the managing board, instead of taking over a finished building, would be stuck with having to complete the building. But I didn't say anything; I was not officially a member of the DOC, and the terms of my presence at their meetings were that I be silent.

David said, "You've got to be fair to the people. You go into the unit and things just aren't finished."

Gwen: "We need a single standard. I have the key to Viv's unit and I invite you to go over and look at it to see the standard. The contractor and architect are done with that."

With that, we were off and running. For the next hour, the members of the DOC talked past one another, each one taking a stand and repeating what they had already said. Gwen kept saying we should all go and look at Viv's unit to see the standard we could expect. Bruce said he was not about to do forty walk-throughs and that Carl was not going to fix everything that fussy owners would complain about. Art, too, worried about "fussy owners." David, Gerard, and Florence tried to speak up for the cohousers, arguing that there were many problems with the units. At one point, I could hold my tongue no longer and suggested that if Art and Gwen's unit were the standard, everybody might be satisfied. "If yours was the worst and everybody else's was better, I think we could all accept that," I said.

Art jumped. It was palpable. He looked at me, startled. Immediately Gwen said "Look at Viv's unit." And with that, everybody went back to repeating what they had already said. At one point, Barbara said, "I think we've developed a group of people who get everything they want." A few such meetings later, a compromise was reached: No one would be allowed to see their unit until Carl was ready to sign off on it. Bruce would then work with the owner(s) to draw up a punch list, which he would present to Carl.

Sometimes I got the feeling that the members of the DOC felt everybody was a bother, as when Barbara said, "I think we've developed a group of people who get everything they want," or when she or someone else on the DOC would say, "Don't let this get out," or "Don't let this get on the email." Similarly, at the managing board meeting on February 6, when we were complaining that our energy consultant said he would charge us one hundred dollars an hour to help us develop a billing formula, someone said to Bert, who was taking the minutes, "All this won't go in the minutes, I hope." And he replied, "Oh, no, there's a lot in my notes that doesn't get into the minutes."

For a commons to work, its members need to know what's going on. If we were to be self- governing, then we all needed to be making decisions based on a common body of knowledge. Transparency is not only a requirement for a successful commons; it is a crucial tool in the development of a commons culture. Information is in itself a commons. Yet, here we were at the birth of our commons, acting like a for-profit corporation, turning our deliberations into secrets and creating a privileged few who would know something about which the rest of us would be kept in the dark.

Knowledge as property—intellectual property, in the public domain—is the current battleground between those who would preserve our commons and what James Boyle, the law professor who has written a defense of the commons, calls "the second enclosure" (Boyle 2003, 45). Although Boyle did his best to simplify the issues, they remain tricky. Intellectual property is a peculiar kind of property. Unlike real estate or the clothes on your back, intellectual property is intangible. As such, it can be simultaneously used by any number of people. Indeed, its value to each of us is enhanced as more and more of us use it. Just think how much more fun it is to burst into a well-known chorus, with your friends all singing together, than to sing some song no one else knows.

Not only is intellectual property enhanced as it enters the public domain to be enjoyed by many; it is, Boyle points out, "nonrival" and "nonexcludable." Space on the internet is so close to infinitely expandable that it does not matter how many books are out there. When I downloaded Boyle's book (which he made available under a Creative Commons license), that did not prevent others from downloading the same book (which I hope you will do, and read it, too). Boyle's point and the point being made by several others (Hyde 2010) is that copyright protections and patent rights are currently being expanded at such a clip that the whole reason for enacting those laws (to increase creative work and creation by rewarding the author and/or inventor) is abrogated by restricting the very creative work that the copyright laws are meant to enhance.

But I digress. My point in raising the issue of the public domain and the current trend to privatize and enclose it is to point out that information and knowledge about what is going on is another station on the axis between the market and the commons. Secrets, hidden deals, and decisions that did not get into the minutes would cut into our commons, while full and accurate minutes broadcast to all of us would help it to grow. Moreover, cliques formed among those in the know that prevented other friendships from forming.

On a Friday at the end of January, a half year after Gwen had promised we could move in, Florence sent out an email letting the East Enders know that they could move their stuff but not themselves into their units: She had just signed a "substantial completion" form. Along with that announcement on our Listserv, she described a visit to the East End:

> Workmen were swarming all over the East End and things are starting to come together. When I arrived, Deb and Jeff and their granddaughter were having a wonderful picnic with Megan in the Wangs' unit, while Tim and Lulu were running errands. Between the kids and the flowers on the window-sills it looked like a real home! As we were munching on spicy noodles and other goodies, a very friendly representative of The Works [the Cambridge Department of Sanitation] arrived with our big, blue, wheeled recycling bins; she smiled and waved as she returned to paste instruction sheets on the top. So, we now have a mailbox and recycling bins—I'll add a couple of trash cans tomorrow! It's beginning to look a lot like home.

In early February, the East Enders, the twelve families who would live in the six town houses and six stacked flats at the eastern end of our site, actually did move in. Among them only Tim and Lulu, for their much-publicized weekend, and David and Joan, for a longer period, had been roofless. The seventeen families who would live in the common house would have to wait until June, and the West Enders would have to wait even longer, until the leaves were falling and the air was crisp and chill again. Through the years, the East Enders' earlier move, coupled with their physical separation from the rest of us down the narrow glade that runs from the East End to the common house, would give the East Enders, and most of the rest of us, a sense that they lived in their own little neighborhood, a special enclave.

By the middle of February, with the East Enders all moved in, I was living in Harriet and Paul's place. The East Enders seemed very pleased—not with everything about their units; there were still long lists of things that needed to be fixed—and one had a good feeling when going over there, as I did each day to pick up my mail and many days to attend a meeting.

There was six-year-old Sally—bright-eyed, petite, and energetic, with a big smile—running down the path to her own house from the one next door, where her friend June lived. Sometimes her older brother was at Paul and Harriet's town house next door, visiting with their two older girls. Kids running from one home to another and somebody you knew always around to say hi or to chat; knowing who was in each unit, especially being able to know something about who was in each unit—such things made the place feel cohesive, a place where you wouldn't be alone and lonely. I was anxious to live there.

I had put myself on a task force to help solve one of the most vexing problems we homeless members were facing. When you had a temporary change of address, the U. S. Postal Service made up a sheet of sticky yellow labels with your temporary address. Every letter came with the yellow label pasted over the old address. By February 1998, some of my letters, the ones that hadn't gotten lost on the way, would arrive with five yellow stickers pasted one on top of the other: one with Linda's address, one with my summer address, one with my fall address, one with Carol's address, and one with Harriet and Paul's address. I thought that I could avoid having my mail travel through yet another post office if I could have it delivered straight to Richdale Avenue. The postmaster said that mail would be delivered to Richdale Avenue as soon as we put up a mailbox. I said it was already up, and I submitted my sixth and final change of address to the post office. I was not living on Richdale Avenue, but at least my mail could be delivered there.

And I could go over there whenever I wanted. One day, when I went by to pick up my mail, Florence came by with some rugs. I helped her carry them up to her third-floor unit. I guess it had crossed her mind to use the chair stair to get them up, because she said something about not using it because it was too cumbersome. She also said that she hadn't lifted weights that day and carrying the rugs would make up for it. It took only a couple of minutes and I got some exercise, too. The day before, I had stopped by at Joan and David's to pick up a newsletter because mine had never gotten to me. They asked me in for some wine and we chatted for an hour or so. I liked that about cohousing—the help that was there without arranging for it, the chats that just happened without your having to call and make plans. And the freedom to say you were in a hurry if you couldn't chat just then. There would always be more opportunities. It wasn't like the usual socializing, where you had to decide to visit for a few hours, usually over a meal, which took time to prepare or cost a lot if you went to a restaurant together. This way, you could just chat for a few minutes and then get on with your day.

Most Mondays, Gwen did a tour of our buildings. We could see the common parts of the buildings that were finished, but we could not go into the units. Then one Monday, Barbara led the tour because Gwen had to be somewhere else. On it were Ted, Jon, and Francesca and Gerard. Later, we were joined by Joan, Lulu, and Olga from the East End. We went down to the basement. When we looked into the mechanical room, Bruce was there talking to the engineer and a woman with a pad—Ted didn't know who she was, but we quickly closed the door. Barbara was saying something about guessing that we shouldn't be there. Francesca and I remarked about how large the laundry room was. The teen room looked small and so did the bike room, considering all the bikes we'd have. I said I thought the storage area was very small and Barbara said she thought it was large. Then I was teased for trying to take every nook and cranny for extra storage. I had given the storage committee report the day before. Later, we walked by the back of the East End town houses and looked into their basement windows: total chaos. Joan said it was even worse than her basement, and I said something about all the people without basements and what were they going to do with their chaos, to which Olga, our most fervent ecologist, replied that they'd have to get rid of it, which would be better.

By the end of March, Epoch had delivered all the units and we were working on the common house punch lists. My brother-in-law, a civil engineer who worked in an architectural firm, offered to do my punch list with me. He wanted to see the drawings and the book of specifications. When I asked, somebody told me that Peter had them. I called him and Kit called back to say that I could go over to their place and pick them up. When I got there, Kit was getting ready for work. She showed me where the plans should have been, but they were not there; neither was the book of specifications. We poked around here and there but could not find them, and then she remembered that she had given them to Francesca. As I was walking back home, I saw Gerard, Francesca's husband, driving by, so I flagged him down and asked him if he knew who had the plans. He said he thought Jon had taken them. I said, "Oh well, Kit is going to email Peter, who is out of town, to find out where they are." A few moments later, Gerard called and said that Jon had borrowed them to do the storage plan. I called Jon, and sure enough, he had them. I said I'd be right over.

When I got there, a deliveryman was holding a package and looking distraught. He had software to deliver to Jon, who hadn't answered when he rang the bell and knocked on the door. He wondered if it would be safe to leave it by the door, next to a sand pail that was sitting there. I agreed to accept the package for Jon. I rang again and again and I knocked. No answer. I thought, How strange, since Jon had said to come right over because they were leaving soon. I imagined that maybe Lori was anxious to leave and they had gone already. So I looked at the East End driveway to see if maybe they were getting into their car. At the end of the driveway, there was a car with people in it. The sun was in my eyes and I couldn't see who it was, so I went over. It was Gerard. I asked him if he had seen Jon and Lori, if he knew whether they had left. He hadn't seen them.

I noticed a young man sitting in the passenger seat and Gerard introduced me to his son. Then he asked if I knew how to put the car in reverse. I did. It was David's Volvo and I had borrowed it once and had figured out how to get the gears into reverse. They drove off and I went to slip a note under Jon's door. By the time I got back to Paul and Harriet's place down the street, there was a message on my answering machine. (I had gotten a landline as soon as I moved to Harriet and Paul's place.) It was from Jon, who said they had been on their third floor the whole time and couldn't hear the bell. So I went back over to get the specifications.

It was an episode to remember. I felt warmed by having that whole group of people who knew one another and could share the silly mix-up, with everybody helping me, however ineptly, to get the plans I wanted. I enjoyed being able to help Gerard with the car, and it was heartwarming to be part of a group that would share in David's generosity as he loaned his Volvo to anyone who needed it. The morning was fun and funny. I thought, IT WORKS! It was hard not to get gushy about the good stuff.

By April, there was still no Certificate of Occupancy for the common house. Carl got angry again and threatened to quit. Some co-housers said that would be a break, that then we could get the place finished properly. On Wednesday, April 15, I had my walk-through with Bruce and put everything that my brother-in-law had noticed on my punch list. On Thursday, *The New York Times* ran a story about us, focusing on our passion for ecology. It was full of mistakes, spelling our names wrong and saying that Barbara was ten years older than she was, but it was positive, pointing out how many researchers from Harvard and elsewhere were studying our project (Brown 1998).

On April 21, Deb called to remind me about a C&CR (conflict and conflict resolution) meeting at Ted and Barbara's that night, and we got to talking about our move-in. She said they had closed, but they couldn't move in. I said, "Yeah, because the certificate of substantial completion hasn't been signed." She asked when I'd found out. I thought back and said that I had heard that the previous Friday. I said that it was possible that we would get in that week but that Carl wouldn't sign off on the common house units until he could sign off on all of them at once. Deb said that the previous week Bruce's assistant had said we could sign off unit by unit. Then I said something about everybody's being afraid of Carl, and Deb said we were like a dysfunctional family with an alcoholic father. "Everybody has to appease him and walk around on tiptoes so that he won't become enraged."

The unit that was holding us all up was Charles and Betsy's. Charles came to the June 9 DOC meeting with two demands. He said his showerhead was too low and his kitchen was badly designed and the LLP should pay for moving his showerhead and changing a cabinet in his kitchen. He said he wanted to set a precedent so the DOC would agree to redesign all the kitchens. I said some of us just needed a place to live and I didn't think the DOC should give in when someone played hardball, because not everybody was in a position to play hardball. Betsy and Charles were living in a rented apartment that they could stay in as long as they wanted, but people who had sold their places and were homeless could not refuse to close until everything was shipshape.

Charles said he thought he was being slandered. That was probably the beginning of years of bad feelings between me and Charles and Betsy. Charles often interrupted and cut me off when I gave a committee report at a general meeting. It was as if he couldn't stand the sound of my voice. Later, Betsy told David and David told me that she wouldn't join any committee that I was on. Day by day our community was becoming pockmarked with similar antipathies, and C&CR was unable to do anything about it. Other communities require members to sign agreements before joining. The agreements address obligations, such as that members contribute a number of hours of work or participation in the community each month; or if one member is having difficulties with another member, the parties talk things over with the help of a mediator if necessary. But at Cambridge Cohousing, some members were staunchly opposed to requirements of any sort, and their strong voices held sway. Here again, we found ourselves on the axis of variation between the rules that keep a commons balanced and the freedom of a marketplace. One could almost think of it as a seesaw between the two poles, and when it came to demands the community might make on our time or talents, our community gave all of its weight to the market's side. We were to be totally free of obligations to our commons, a freedom that weakened our commons without strengthening any individual among us; it was like those who in the middle of a pandemic claim the freedom to refuse vaccination while a virus attacks their community.

The day I finally moved in, I was too busy to take notes. It was in June,1998, a year later than Gwen had promised I could move in. I was euphoric to be moving my stuff and myself into the place I would live in, perhaps for the rest of my life. My bedroom was small, and there was no linen closet in the unit; in fact, I don't think that Bruce had designed a linen closet in any of the flats. I had decided to solve that problem by using the space under my bed for linens. It took a lot of shopping, but finally, on the Web, I found a double bed with drawers underneath. It came wrapped in big boxes and it took me several days to put it together, even with the help of an electric screwdriver I borrowed from Paul.

As I worked on the bed, I remembered the day decades earlier when Dick and I had bought a big red fire engine for Harry's third birthday. It came wrapped in boxes, just like the bed. I'd started trying to put it together but was flummoxed; Dick was even worse at that sort of thing. Angry at being forced to finish assembling the fire engine, I called the department store and told the person on the phone that what I had bought was the fire engine displayed on the floor of the store, not a box of parts. The next day, the store sent someone to put it together. I won that battle, but, as we all know, manufacturers won the war. Now all customers can hope for are clear instructions on the boxes of parts that they buy.

It would take the better part of the next few years for me to get down to the bottoms of the last barrels and boxes. I kept hoping to find Dick's mother's Waterford crystal and my KLH radio, but they never turned up, and the mover reminded me that when I'd cut through the shrink wrap to get my winter clothes, I had lost all chance of recovering missing items or their value. I totted it up to one more lesson in the art of losing.

By early June of 1998, all but two units in the common house were occupied. The West Enders would have to wait until fall. Gwen and Art would join them. They had sold their Cambridge condo and were commuting from their summer home on Cape Cod. I met Gwen going down in the elevator one day. She said she had timed it wrong; she would have to put their stuff in storage for a few weeks until their unit would be ready. I said, "Well, maybe now you can see what it felt like for the rest of us."

"Oh," she said, her tone one of pride and self-congratulation sprinkled with instruction, "I treat it like a vacation." I thought of Kipling's words (Kipling 1886):

> The toad beneath the harrow knows
> Exactly where each tooth-point goes.
> The butterfly upon the road
> Preaches contentment to that toad.

Our vision statement imagined a diverse community, but for all our trying, we didn't get much of the kind of diversity that most cohousing communities hope for—differences in class, race, and ethnicity. Like those in other cohousing communities across the country, almost all of us were from white European backgrounds and, except for the tenants of the two units the Cambridge Housing Authority bought and rented out as subsidized units, we were all middle-class and all college-educated. That didn't prevent Gwen from claiming in the Spring 1997 issue of *Cohousing,* the national cohousing journal, that "[o]ur goals for age, income, racial, and ability diversity are substantially met." What few of us realized at the time was that through our helter-skelter process of completing our buildings, we were creating a different but critical dimension of inequality—those who had and those who had not experienced rooflessness on our way to cohousing.

Several types of cohousers did not have to experience homelessness. They were the renters, who could negotiate lease extensions with their landlords; those well-heeled enough to be able to own their old homes and their new ones in Cambridge Cohousing simultaneously; those who had trouble selling their homes and did not manage to do so until it was close to move-in time; and, finally, the ones Gwen worried about, who ignored her exhortations to sell their homes. They continued to live in their old homes even if that meant not having the down payment to take possession of their new ones the moment their units were ready. Even among the homeless, there were differences. Some owned second homes, where they could spend the summer and store their things. Others, like me, had to put everything we owned in storage, keeping out only whatever could fit into one or two suitcases. Like many other forms of social diversity, the rooflessness some of us experienced would be invisible to those who had not suffered it. Those who had not been roofless for a year or more did not seem to know about or sympathize with those of us whose lives would never recover the losses, some material, but most psychological, physical, and even practical when our careers were handicapped.

For me, that year of rooflessness left permanent scars, but it had one benefit. In a survey of cohousers, the Cohousing Research Network asked respondents about the benefits of cohousing. One of the most frequent replies was that respondents felt they had experienced personal growth by living in cohousing. In a way, though my health deteriorated and my career was pretty much ended by that year of homelessness, I did grow in at least one way.

What I found myself doing after months of rooflessness was just responding to my most urgent needs, just trying each day to put one foot in front of the other, just getting from one day to the next. Of course, even though we called ourselves homeless, our situation was totally different from those who were truly homeless. We knew our homelessness would end, even though each time we thought we were close to that day, it was postponed. We knew where our things were even if some of them would be lost forever. We had friends and relatives who had taken us in and would again if called upon. We could afford to rent temporary housing. But still, for me, a corner of the curtain on that desperate and horrific world of the homeless was lifted, if ever so slightly.

I can only imagine what happens to one's sense of self when one cannot surround one's nakedness with more than the clothes on one's back. Sometimes I see a homeless person pushing a shopping cart filled with miscellaneous stuff. Perhaps they are the lucky ones; they still have stuff to push around. But what if you have no place at all to put your stuff, especially your photos of people you once loved and who loved you? (If they were still around and they had a place, they'd take you in.) Who are you then? How can you get out of the hole you fell into? It's hard for homelessness not to lead to hopelessness. Imagine going for a job interview when you haven't the clothes to dress for success. And what's the point of a job interview when they say "Don't call us, we'll call you" and you have no number to leave with them? Now, when I pass a homeless person, I am much more likely to have a little better understanding of what that person is going through. I almost admire anybody who can keep going without a home.

I did not miss the irony that the loss of my stable home occurred because I was trying to have a home in a commons, in a stable community. As I write this, I am struck by something David Beasley said when his organization, the UN World Food Programme, won the 2020 Nobel Peace Prize. All it would take to feed those at risk for one year is five billion dollars (Beasley 2020). That is what Amazon CEO Jeff Bezos makes every two weeks (Allcot 2021). One hundred and fifty million people are homeless worldwide. There is no figure for what it would take to house them, but in 2013 HUD estimated that it would take twenty billion dollars to end homelessness in the United States. The Center for American Progress notes that this is "less than half of what we spend each year on weight loss and self-improvement" (Steenland 2013). Imagine how easily some of the world's most intractable problems might yield to a world where the balance between the market and the commons shifted even slightly toward the commons.

Nine

We're All In

1998

During the first half of 1998, the east enders enjoyed their new homes and, along with the rest of us, urged our developers and contractor toward completion. In June 1998, the common house residents moved in, and, finally, by Thanksgiving, a full year and a half later than promised, we were all at home in Cambridge Cohousing.

Up until then, our focus had been on constructing our buildings. We did little to intentionally construct the communal life we would share, which was, after all, the whole reason we were constructing our buildings. Those among us who thought we should be focusing more on our life as a community had a rough time trying to get the attention of the others.

Nonetheless, over time, our community did take on patterns and processes as we pooled our resources and began acting in concert. Shortly after we moved into the common house, we put up a whiteboard by the elevator for notices. If one of us was in the hospital, someone, usually Francesca, would put a note on the whiteboard. Newborn babies were announced there, and when they or anyone else came home from the hospital, someone would put up a list so that we could sign up to take them dinner for a week or so. Thus, as we took up residence bit by bit, we began acting like a community bit by bit.

As is true for other condominiums, our bylaws called for a managing board to take care of our property. One of its first jobs was to hire a managing company. Continuing our penny-wise and pound-foolish pattern, we chose the Ford over the Cadillac—and got an Edsel. Waverly, the company we chose, was pretty much a three-person operation and was as new to its job as we were to ours.

An even larger problem than our inexperience and theirs was the lack of common knowledge about how to build and govern a community. There was not much to go on. Joan had bought several copies of *On Conflict and Consensus* (Butler and Rothstein 1991) for the community, but its spiral-bound sixty-four pages gave little guidance. Our biggest problem was that any one of us could veto any proposal by raising a red card. Like the UN, with a veto power in the hands of the five permanent members, we were hampered by each of us having the right to raise a red card and thus defeat any proposal. In fact, if someone didn't like a proposal that was coming down the pike, all that person had to do was threaten to red-card it and the person or the group that was preparing it would give up.

Nonetheless, we did come to many agreements. Just as the question of private gardens emerged where the commons met the market, so, too, one of the first issues the managing board had to deal with emerged at the boundary between our private and our common worlds: things left in front of unit doors. It did not affect the town houses, with their patches of garden by their front doors. But, like zits on adolescent faces, boots, doormats, benches, shopping carts, and kids' skates gradually took residence by the front doors in the East End stacked flats shortly after residents moved in.

I was clued into the problem when Kit complained of Jen's stuff. Jen was a collector of many things—magazines, brochures, newspapers, jackets, shoes. As she unpacked, treasures for which she had no place inside her unit began to appear outside her front and rear doors, in the front hall lobby, and in the basement. That made Kit cross. He lived on the first floor, Jen on the third. Each floor in the East End stacked flats had two units, a two-bedroom to the left, Jen's side, where she lived with her daughter Jennifer, and a three-bedroom to the right, occupied on the second and third floors by single women—Janet and Florence. Frank, who lived below Jen, also stored his outdoor footwear on the landing. Florence, Jen's floor mate, didn't seem to be bothered by the stuff Jen was accumulating on their landing, and Janet, Frank's floor mate, hardly seemed to notice his boots.

What sparks one person's radar is different from what sparks another's, and it is possible that this issue might not have reached decision-making proportions had it not been for the blips and squeaks on Kit's radar. When Kit could stand the stuff in the halls no longer, he brought the issue to the managing board. We managing board members were new at our job, but not so new that we didn't know what to do with a problem too barbed to handle. We threw the matter to our managing company. The managing company, almost as inexperienced as we were, threw it to the insurance company, whose agent said it was the fire department, not the insurance company, that said that halls must be free of anything that might impede the egress of inhabitants or the ingress of firefighters into a blazing, smoke-filled building. The agent was quick to point out that because of the increased risk of damage to persons and property, the company would have to raise our rates if we did not get all that stuff off the floor landings and common passageways.

Threatened with probable increased costs and possible death by tripping, I, as the first vice chairperson of the managing board, was asked to draw up a set of rules for the storage of personal property in public spaces. These rules were published in the next newsletter. I thought I did a fine job of succinctly proposing a simple policy: "As storage of personal items creates a hazard in the case of fire and also in fairness to those who, for lack of onsite storage space, are paying for offsite storage, we will adopt the following policy: All personal property must be removed from public passageways within two weeks of moving in. If personal property is left out, the owner will receive a warning letter. One week later the objects will be removed."

At the May 1998 general meeting, held in the basement of the East End flats, we discussed those rules. No one objected to the content of the proposal, but there were serious objections to its tone: It was too authoritative, and some among us wanted to have nothing to do with rules or authorities. One person said that our by-laws already addressed the use of common areas, so we didn't need a separate proposal; another objected to the level of detail in the proposed enforcement procedure; to which someone else pointed out that we needed enforcement in order to avoid an increase in our insurance costs. Someone else noted that problems only came to the attention of the managing board after they had been going on for weeks or months and the proposal only addressed issues that had finally come to the managing board. Joan proposed that we form a task force to revise the proposal, and David, Jen, and Karen volunteered to bring a more gently worded proposal to the next meeting.

Several iterations later, the policy agreed upon called for the managing company to tag offending items, which then had to be removed by their owners or be confiscated by the managing company. Over the years, no matter how many times we asked each other to remove such items, nothing, not hopes and fears exercises, not special task forces, not visiting firefighters, not various enforcement schemes—nothing!—could keep the stuff from reappearing on the stair landings of the stacked flats and outside the doorways of units in the common house. Then for many years, the matter was dropped. By 2018, almost everyone had a mat and maybe another item or two by their doorway. No one said anything, and our insurance rates were not increased because of it. It was looking as though the smarter approach would have been to follow Calvin

Coolidge's governing style: Do nothing, for, as he famously said, "if you see ten troubles coming down the road, you can be sure that nine will run into the ditch before they reach you." But by 2018, big changes were in the works. Cambridge Cohousing instituted its own constitutional convention, and a new governing structure empowered a 2020 Fire Safety subcircle to work with the Cambridge Fire Department to institute new rules. This appeared draconian to some, but the new subcircle seems to have the power to make its rules stick.

The beginnings of a more orderly system of self-government began in June 1998, when the common house residents moved in. Practices and procedures that might have fallen easily into place in the East End for the six families living in the stacked flats and the six others living in the town houses now had to be discussed and decided on by those living in the seventeen units in the common house. Not only were we greater by five in our number of units but, as we had only two units with the ground-level outdoor sitting space that all but four of the East End units had, and as we used the stairs or the elevator to get to our units, we were less likely than the East Enders to encounter each other for casual chats and agreements about how to do this or that. Moreover, most of the community's common facilities were located in the common house and we had to come to agreement on how they would be used. That included our two kids' rooms, the music room, the rec room, the library, our two guest rooms, the living room, the dining room, the kitchen, lawn, patio, and flowering borders. Even though all of these facilities belonged to the East Enders as much as they did to those living in the common house, the latter's proximity to them in practice made their care and management fall more heavily on the common house residents. The East End had only the workshop and the vegetable garden to organize and maintain.

We needed systems for storage, for making sure all the doors and windows in the common house were locked after dark, for getting our garbage and recycling barrels to the curb each week, for the work we would do together fixing up and maintaining our common spaces, for the meals we would prepare and eat together a few times a week, and, of course, for changing the lightbulbs in our common rooms and halls.

As the vice chair of the managing board, I became the go-to person for a slew of tasks, small and large, which ate up my days, leaving me little time for my paid job—professor of sociology, teaching three classes each semester. Almost every day, I had to attend to something that had to be decided or fixed. At least once a week, something unexpectedly lovely would happen and I'd know why we had gone to so much trouble to build our cohousing community, but at least once a week there'd be something so disappointing, I wondered why we had bothered.

June 2, for example, began with no hot water. I called Gwen and the managing company. Gwen blamed the city for turning off the water and not turning it back on. She said she'd call the person responsible. We had hot water again by noon the following day. Then Jen called; she wanted to know if she was covered by the cohousing insurance policy. I tried to explain to her that the managing board bought insurance for the common areas but that each of us had to buy homeowner's insurance for our own unit and its contents. She thought I was wrong and asked for the name of our insurance company so she could talk to someone there. I gave her the name of the broker but suggested she speak to Carla, who was handling insurance for the board. A few minutes later, Carla called to tell me that Jen had said, "Diane doesn't know anything."

Though I thought she was probably right, at least when it came to insurance, I was still smarting when Jeff knocked at my door with the addendum to his equity loan that he wanted me to look at. I told Jeff about Jen's insult. We agreed that it would be a good idea to bring it to the C&CR committee. Jen was, after all, one of a number of cohousers who at that time were sending emails to our Listserv about our manners, suggesting that we speak to one another "in the cohousing spirit."

We all adopt a different manner and tone depending on whom we are speaking to—friends, family members, our bosses, or our subordinates. I thought being a commoner in a commons called for the friendly voice of equals. But some of those who had been renters spoke in the demanding voice they must previously have used with the superintendent of their building, or their landlord: Something was wrong and they wanted it fixed pronto. They didn't seem to understand that as commoners in a commons, they were as responsible for anything that didn't work as anyone else and that the ones who were trying to get things fixed were volunteers, doing their best to straighten things out in spite of a building fraught with problems.

At a meeting of the C&CR committee, I grumbled about the complainers, saying that it really irked me that people treated those of us who were struggling to get this place up and running as if they were Bell Atlantic (our telephone company). To which Deb replied that we shouldn't treat the folks at BA as if they were BA. "They are just poor underpaid folk who work there and have no power," she said. Ted and Deb agreed that there was no way to get people to treat each other more civilly. I hoped they were wrong, but I had nothing to suggest.

On June 7, 1998, the common house residents held an organizing meeting. We dashed through some decisions about how we would share and manage our commons more quickly than most of us chose meals from a restaurant menu. Often, someone would identify a problem that needed a plan; usually, the same person would suggest a solution. We'd try it for a while, and if it worked, it would become our practice; if not, we'd try something else until we hit upon a solution that did work.

For example, there was the laundry room in the basement, with three washers and two dryers, which those in the seventeen common house units shared. We decided that we wouldn't schedule our turns in the laundry room as other cohousing communities had done; we'd just go down when it suited us and see how that worked. It worked well. We thought that when you got there, if all the machines were in use, you could leave your phone number so that someone could call you when the machines were free. That didn't work. Today, we just keep going down until a machine is available—usually, it doesn't take more than one or two tries. If you wouldn't be down in time to move your wash from the washer to the dryer, we said you should leave a note with drying instructions. That didn't work, either, but leaving a basket for your damp clothes did. We decided to keep plant-potting tools in the laundry room, saying that everybody should clean up after themselves. That didn't work, and we have no common potting place. We needed an iron and ironing board—Kate said she'd contribute a board and Sally said she'd contribute an iron.

There were also security problems. We needed to keep the doors and windows locked at night. The building was still being finished and the workers left windows open and doors unlocked. We decided that we needed to put signs up to remind everybody to close windows and lock doors. Also, we had to be careful not to leave hoses around, because if we did, the workmen would take them. Eventually, we worked out a schedule where those in the common house and those in the West End would take turns checking the windows and doors on the first floor and basement, a chore the East Enders never have had to take on.

Then there was garbage: The barrels needed to be taken to the curb every Sunday evening. The Cambridge Department of Public Works wanted us to get a contractor and a Dumpster but had agreed to a trial period during which we would put our barrels out on the curb like other homeowners. We had to be very careful or the city wouldn't take our garbage. We decided that each floor would take turns getting the barrels out and that we'd start the following week with the second floor; Carla would write up the schedule. We were reminded once more to break up boxes and tie them together. We had to recycle—no Styrofoam or trash in the recycling. What about composting? someone asked. We needed a volunteer to manage it.

We needed to keep the common areas clean. At first, we tried to take care of it all by ourselves: In the common house, those on each floor were assigned to clean their own lobby area and the stairs to the floor below; additionally, each of us was supposed to adopt an area in the common house that we would superintend and clean. We still do our own landscaping, gardening, and cooking, but, as many areas became orphans and those who were taking care of their areas became annoyed with those who were not taking care of theirs, we decided to have a cleaning service come in once a week to clean the indoor common areas in the common house.

Francesca had put up hanging plants in the veranda that needed regular watering. The trees needed watering, too, including the ones the city had planted along the street. The buzzer system didn't work, so guests had to call from the corner store to let us know they had arrived (still no cell phones). Did the library need to be kept locked? On and on it went. We agreed to meet again to see how our plans were working.

On June 10, The Boston Globe reported that ten inches of rain had fallen over a period of forty-eight hours. The basements in the common house and East End flooded. We complained to the developers, but Art said it was a one-hundred-year storm and there was no way to build so that once in one hundred years there wouldn't be flooded basements. Gwen said the flooding was the responsibility of the cohousers because the common house now belonged to the LLP. Florence said that it didn't really matter who owned the buildings because we were either covered by the construction insurance policy or the condo insurance and that neither of them covered water damage. I said that wasn't the only issue; we had to assess responsibility for future damage and see what we could do to prevent it.

On June 18, I looked over the flood damage with Gwen. She showed me how the water would be diverted to a well by the back door if we built up the blacktop another four inches. She said the French drain should carry the water off. I pointed out how high the water was in the well by the door. She said that was the height of the water table.

The next day, Gary, the maintenance man from the managing company, came to inspect the building with Francesca and me. At the back door, we noticed that some blacktop had just been added. Gary said it would make water damage worse because it was graded toward the building instead of away from it. I pointed to the well by the door, which was almost overflowing, and said Gwen had told me that the French drain should carry the water away. Gary said that was not a French drain. Francesca said anybody who had owned a house knew what a French drain was. I had owned three houses by then and I wasn't about to admit that I didn't know what a French drain was. I ventured a guess. "Then it's a dry well?" "No," said Gary, "a dry well would be dry."

Later, I asked my sister, who had been living in the same house for forty years, to tell me what a French drain was. She didn't know, either, so we asked her husband, the civil engineer. He explained that a French drain is a ditch around a building meant to carry rainwater away from the building. We never did find out what kind of a draining system we were supposed to have. All we knew was that it wasn't working. Some of us got together to wash the walls down with a Clorox solution to attack the mildew that was beginning to grow black and fuzzy on our walls.

Over the July Fourth weekend, on my way to visit friends on Martha's Vineyard, I ran into Carl, our contractor, on the ferry and said something to him about our air-conditioning not working. When I came back the following Tuesday evening, people were sitting around the common house patio. I thought it was late to be sitting around, but I went to join them to see what was going on. Barbara and Francesca were sitting together. They welcomed me back and we hugged.

I felt a glow; I was home. It wasn't Dick's "Hi, honey" and big bear hug with candles and the table all set for dinner, but I wasn't as lonely as I had been. Francesca interrupted my musings, saying I should have stayed away longer, noting that Kate was making a fuss about my shelves and the bookcase that I had left in the way of her bike. I apologized and said I'd tried to be careful to keep them to one side, not to block the way to the door, and she said it was hard to get her bike in. I said I was sorry. Then Betsy said, "Here's a suggestion: Leave a note like I did when I borrowed the gloves and Clorox and then Francesca just came up and asked for it and that was fine."

"I thought of doing that," I said, "but I was going away, so there would have been no answer if someone had knocked on my door."

After complaining about my shelves some more, Kate turned to the noise of Bert's air conditioner above her bedroom window. I said that I couldn't see how we could forbid air conditioners if the HVAC wasn't working, and Kate stuck her nose within an inch of mine and shouted that their air-conditioning was on cool and they had all their windows open. I said I didn't know about that, and somehow Kate let up. I went upstairs to my unit and saw that Carla had left a message on my phone. She said that Bert said I had given him permission to have an air conditioner. I thought, Well, what I said was that if it was me and there was no air-conditioning and I was getting sick, I'd go ahead and get an air conditioner. I had said that as a fellow cohouser, not as vice chair of the managing board, but I thought, I'd better be careful about that, realizing my words were carrying more weight than I was used to.

The next day, there was a message on my phone from Gwen. Carl had called her and was angry that she hadn't told him that the air-conditioning wasn't working. He was getting the air-conditioning people to fix it and give him a report. Then Bobby, who worked for Carl, was at my door with the air- conditioning people "You talked to Carl, WOW!" They fussed and fiddled but couldn't make it work.

That day, Gwen put a note in each person's cubby. It let us know that on July 7 and 8 several technicians would be around, trying to get the system to work. One would be Mark Kelley, who had designed the system. Gwen said he "would like cohousers to be assured that the system is both high quality and straightforward, and that the adjustments being made at this time are the normal ones that any system needs." She said it was his "intent to have the A. C. fully operational this week. When it is running [highlighted] the need for window air conditioning units will no longer exist."

It took more than a decade to get the HVAC to work properly, and to this day, some units are never cool enough in the summer or warm enough in the winter. At first, because of our desire to be green and free of the neighbor-disturbing noise, we tried to do without individual air conditioners. But when it turned out that the best our system could do was air cooling, not air-conditioning, we relaxed our rules, and many people, some with allergies, bought air conditioners. Others still use electric heaters to dispel the cold of winter.

Kids in Cohousing

For children, cohousing can be wonderful. No sooner were my granddaughters, Anna and Isabel, here on a visit than they were knocking on doors, especially on Lori's and Gail's doors downstairs to see if they could come out and play. Once when we went to the garden to pick some peas, June invited the girls up to see her toys. Isabel came down a few minutes later, looking a bit sad. She was younger than the other two girls and she might have felt left out. A few minutes later, Anna came down all dressed up with a crown and a wand that June wanted to give her.

On the other hand, different parenting styles could lead to difficulties. "How do we deal with kids whose parents practice lenient discipline? Are we to discipline them?" one parent asked on our Listserv, noting, "These same kids do not listen when telling them about safety and respecting other kids' safety and welfare. Whose responsibility is it? The community can only do so much."

Once when I was in the glade with Anna and Isabel, Betsy saw us from her balcony and, without asking if I would watch them, sent her two younger children down to join us. When we were ready to leave, I had to ask her older daughter, who happened to walk by just then, to go up and let Betsy know that I would not be able to keep watching her two-year-old and four-year-old. Betsy must have done something of the sort often, because another note on the Listserv said, "I suggest that: If a parent is leaving his/her child and the child is in the presence of another adult, that parent should specifically ask them to watch their child. Not assume that since someone is there, your child is safe. That way we can be clear about expectations."

There was also the issue of bikes, trikes, and other toys being left in the halls and on the lawn, which prompted one parent to suggest a set of rules for bike and toy storage. That didn't sit well with Betsy, who replied:

> As a common house resident with small children, I'm not very happy with the rigid tone of these rules and ask that you think them through a little more. Common house kids have no other accessible space for these items, and they've been told that if they leave their items on the grounds (by the fence along the outside

spine for example) that they are signaling that they can be used
by all children. (West and East End kids signal that their things are
"off- limits" by putting them on their patios or other semi-private
outdoor space.)

In mid-July, the carpet on the stairway from the first to the second floor was deeply stained. At the next managing board meeting,
Francesca raised it as a problem and Betsy explained: "What had
happened was, I was walking up the stairs with three kids and Adam
behind me, so I didn't notice that he was dripping the Popsicle. It
was that neon blue; anything else would have come out—they're
water-soluble— but neon blue! I tried using a rug cleaner on it; that
has always taken out anything that spilled, but not this. So I'm
wondering what Carla used; maybe she used something that set it."

Francesca replied, "Just water, I think. That's why we need rules
about where food can be eaten; there should be a rule that you can't
eat on the stairs."

"But," said Betsy, "he wasn't eating it; he was just carrying it."

Francesca: "I have some stuff at work that takes out stains. I'll
bring it home."

Betsy: "The carpet was supposed to be stain-proofed."

At the next general meeting, on July 26, among the announcements that started the meeting was one from Francesca, for IDA,
about spills in common areas: "Kids may spill, if carrying food
through; watch kids and clean up." In the discussion that followed,
someone said that we needed to find ways to thank others for what
they were giving, but David said he was praised too much. "All I did
was cut the grass. I enjoyed it—it hardly took fifteen minutes—but
the praise was almost too much." And then he said that it was the
people who do too much who were the problem. Francesca said that
some people said they felt guilty about her doing so much work,
even though she enjoyed the gardening. Phyllis said that she worked
harder on group cleaning than on her own place. Lyn said, "This

is just a terrible time for me; I can't do anything." And David said that was just fine and encouraged her to do nothing.

At the general meeting on August 23, Don brought in a proposal from the governance committee about working in teams: All residents, including children, would be expected to be on a work team. We needed to agree on how much work each resident owed the community; work would be organized by the various committees—kitchen, IDA, grounds, etc.—so that they could decide what work needed to be done each month and organize it. Art said we needed a concrete plan to get the work done and that the managing board needed to get volunteers or hire someone to do the work in order to maintain the value of our property. Gwen said there were still many unanswered questions, such as how much time everyone owed the community. We all agreed that people enjoy doing what they are good at and that we needed to fill gaps in tasks according to what we were good at. Fran said that while it was important that all contributions be valued, we must get stuff done. Jeff said he would rather pay for work than have some feel they had to do it and resent it. And Kate wanted us to avoid hiring for a year if possible. The governance committee said it would meet again in a week and that the heads of committees should make lists of tasks and post them on the bulletin board, allowing space for volunteers to sign up. Someone noted that work on the lawn had been posted for weeks but nothing had been done.

Trash Talk and Freeloaders

The friction between those who did the work and those who created work for them to do came to a head over trash and the need to break down packing boxes. From the moment a cohouser put out a box that wasn't broken down, trash was a story of success and failure. Over the years, we have succeeded in developing a system that works for getting the trash barrels from our trash enclosure to the street each week, but we still have trouble with people who put garbage in the recycle bins.

The hope, of course, is that people who choose to live in a cohousing community are the kind of people who don't want to be freeloaders and will be self-policing. But that has not proved to be the case. For example, from the start there were some members of the community who could not be bothered to cut up their packing boxes, giving rise to the following angry email from Stew, whose town house overlooked the West End garbage enclosure:

Subject: box culprits Sun, 20 Sep 1998

This message is for west enders and common-house folks only. East enders can just relax and be amused at my little rant. It's now 8:10 p.m. on Sunday evening and once again a noble soul is outside in the trash area tearing and cutting up boxes, tying them with string, and hauling them to the curb for recycling—Gerard, Chuck, and myself to name a few. Week after week people continue to simply dump boxes in the enclosure, merrily walking away, either ignorant of the work they are foisting on someone else or simply lazily and sneakily pretending nobody will notice. Well, goddamn it, cut it OUT! This is ridiculous! We're supposed to be intelligent, respectful, community-minded people. I'm sorry to lose my cool here, but I really am pissed off. Since I have the pleasure of a perfect view of the trash area, I'm going to start paying attention to who's putting what where. I'll try to be polite if I see some box culprits, but don't count on it. Whoever you are, you should bloody well know by now that your boxes don't magically appear on the curb all cut and tied. And here, for the zillionth time, is the ONLY way the city will take your boxes: cut up, stacked, and tied or taped in a liftable pile no larger than 3 feet on a side.

End of rant (though I'm going to repeat myself at the next general meeting for the non-emailed amongst us).

Viv added her two cents:

Subject: Re: box culprits

Thank you, Stew, for saying what I've been grumbling about to anyone who'd listen. About last night, I also learned that Diane and Bert packed up the remaining boxes with Styrofoam peanuts that some folk(s) put there, maybe hoping they'd also disappear. The city only takes those at the drop-off recycling place and so, I believe Bert now has them in his car ready to be driven over there. Thank you, Diane and Bert. Perhaps this is one email that needs to be printed and posted or placed in everyone's box. (Where I lived before the management paid a maintenance crew to do all the trash work . . . is that what it will take for us to learn to deal with our own trash?)

And Gerard:

Subject: trash talk

Friends in the West End and CH:

Thanks, Stew and Viv, and all those helpers. One of the quiet ones is Tony Brown. And Ted did a lot this week. But we need a stronger system. It is not right to have one person going out there on Sunday and putting in a lot of time and effort and then someone else showing up on his/her own and doing some more and wondering who did the first bit and who may be coming later, etc., a series of grumbling freelancers. We need teams, people who show up TOGETHER at the same time and work cheerfully together. Some people just do not want to be bothered with trash, garbage, recycling, or refuse (which is that which we refuse or reject). But they must be made aware of some basic rules so that they no longer burden others. Cardboard is one. NO PLASTIC BAGS in the recycling is another. Clean out your smelly beer bottles. Don't dump.

• • •

It wasn't all trouble. One day toward the end of June as I was walking through our gate, I passed Lyn, who was moving into her new home on the first floor of the common house. "I'm exhausted," she said, "never felt so tired in my life." I invited her to take a break and join me for lunch. She said she was very happy to be here, couldn't figure out why everybody wasn't living in cohousing. She had lived in her other place for fourteen years and knew only two of her neighbors, neither of them very well. Now here she was, just moved in and enjoying lunch with a neighbor.

Later she came up to use my phone. I had just taken some salmon out of the freezer and said there was enough for two and would she join me for dinner? She hesitated, then demurred, saying she didn't want to impose. I said it wasn't an imposition, that I would enjoy her company, and so she agreed to join me, but, as it turned out, her friend Jay came and we all went out to eat at a Chinese restaurant nearby. Lyn said again how nice it was that we could share a meal on the spur of the moment.

On September 26, I invited my writers' group to meet at my home so I could show it off and talk about cohousing. Kay and Ruth were the first to arrive. They were full of oohs and "aahs." "It is beautiful," "so light," "so big," "so airy." I was pleased. I had rushed around all morning to fix up the place, but I modestly said, "It is a work in progress." The office was still a mess. I had hung a couple of masks from my collection, but lots of stuff was still helter-skelter on the long east-facing desk. My printer was still on the floor and Dick's dad's dictionary stand kept getting bumped into. Still, with its two walls of books, it looked great.

My guests asked lots of questions.

"Are there any units available?"

"No, we've been sold out for about two years." (And I told about the *Globe* story and how we sold out a few months later.)

"How many units?"

"Forty-one."

"How much did they cost?"

"From about sixty thousand dollars for the studios to about three hundred and fifty thousand for the large town houses."

"What's co about it? What's the difference between this place and any other?"

I explained that we were self-managed and that we worked together to maintain the place and that we did many things together and had begun having a couple of meals together each week. I was amazed at how positive everybody was and at how many times they asked me if any units were available. Whatever our troubles in getting this place going, we had accomplished something.

A few days later, Lori's seven-foot Steinway arrived. It was built in 1900 and was in concert condition. Gerard, Karen, Florence, Bert, and I were working in the library after a pizza dinner when it came. The cost of moving it was supported by many volunteers, and the community agreed to keep it tuned and insured. Someone went to get Fran to play it. But Fran was tired and begged off, saying she had had a hard day.

The next morning, on my way down to the basement, I heard the piano, so I went to see who was playing. It was Fran. "A good piano," she declared.

Conflict and Its Resolution

By the end of 1998, some of us were annoying others so much that at least one of us threatened to call the police. That was Stew, the facilitator of the managing board. His neighbor, Frank, had taken up drumming and was often playing his drums just when Stew and his wife were trying to get their kids to nap. The C&CR committee stepped in and was, in this single instance, successful. It proposed a plan to turn the teen room into a music room, and at the next general meeting a consensus was reached. It was a small room that the teens never used and it was next to the garage and under the kitchen, so no one was likely to be disturbed by sounds coming from it. C&CR also distributed a list of guidelines about what to do if your neighbor was disturbing you:

Considerations Concerning Disturbances

Definition of a disturbance: If someone's enjoyment of their home or common spaces is greatly reduced by noise, odors, or other invasive behavior, the person who is thus annoyed has suffered a disturbance.

What to do if you are disturbed:

First: Speak as soon as possible to the person who is annoying you. Let him or her know you are being disturbed. Try to find an accommodation.

Second: If for any reason you find it difficult to discuss the disturbance with the person causing it, or if negotiations seem to break down, bring the matter to C&CR as soon as possible.

DO NOT:

Harbor grievances.

Bring the matter before Cambridge civil authorities (i.e. police or such) until you are sure that every cooperative avenue for solution has been thoroughly tried.

Threaten to sue or to call in civil authorities. Make threats of any kind.

Rationale: The point of cohousing is to create an environment for community life which is peaceful and in which consideration for each other is paramount. Peace, quiet, harmony, and safety take precedence over any individual's right to noisy, dangerous, or otherwise disturbing self-expression.

As 1998 came to an end, Francesca was organizing our first art show; she was also taking care of our guest room sign-ups and putting together a pamphlet listing all of our furniture donations to our common spaces. Lori and Frank were working on a list of advocates, people who would help out if you let them know you were having trouble with something and would like support. They reminded everyone that there was a community support meeting once a month. Many of us had adopted a room in the common house to keep clean, but some spaces were still orphans and some of the adopted spaces hadn't been cleaned in a long time. Dogs were a problem: There were complaints that their poop was found on the lawn. Dog owners had formed a task force and the owners asked to be told if droppings were found. Fran, its leader, said, "Spread the word, don't spread the turd." There was a problem with the dining room, which was so noisy that many people didn't come to meals. Trash was still a problem, with people not cutting up their packing boxes and putting garbage in the recycling, but we had solved one problem: When we put out the trash, we put deposit bottles in a special receptacle, so then the scavengers who would come by and leave a mess as they went through the containers, looking for deposit bottles, could just empty the special receptacle.

A dedication was being planned. Gwen suggested that we all write down everything that we were angry about and throw all the notes into a blazing fire. Some of us were angered by the suggestion. We had something more like South Africa's truth and reconciliation commission in mind. But nothing came of that, either.

A dedication task force organized a small ceremony, and one fine November morning we all gathered at the East End parking area. We each had a drum, bell, or tambourine that Frank had supplied. He showed me a simple tattoo on the drum I had taken. "Just use this part of your hand," he said, pointing to a place on my palm. I followed his instructions and he went on to coach someone else. Frank is elfin—a small man who manages his world in mysterious ways. As is true of many of us, he has a doctorate. I don't know what his is in, but his work has to do with alternatives of all kinds—health, schools, organizations. Shortly after he joined the group, he acted as our facilitator at the core meetings; then he set up a group to teach others how to facilitate, and they became the facilitators for all the general meetings. For a while, he ran a sharing circle on a Friday evening each month. At the second one, people were talking about how stressed-out they were, how they had no time for anything. Frank said he'd solved all that. He has a lot of time, even though he has many businesses. I can't remember what he advised those who were stressed.

I was still banging on my drum when I noticed that the others had raised their hands, which was our signal for quiet. Frank struck his drum three times and said that would be the signal for quiet. By this time, everybody had some rhythm instrument. Marilyn handed out a map of our compound, showing stopping places. At each one, Marilyn announced, we would dip our branch with pine needles into the bowl of water and sprinkle it over the ground. No one said "holy water" or "hallowed ground"—we seemed too playful, self-deprecating, and irreverent for that—but we had the feel that we were consecrating our place.

We ended in our dining room, where a few people said what Cambridge Cohousing meant to them. Sis was one of the gaggle of girls, whose ages ranged from nine to eleven, who moved in with us. She said, "When I first saw my unit, I was really sad. I thought it would be much bigger than it was. But after we moved in, I found that I had all the space in my unit, in Claire's unit, and in the common house. My place is really big."

"With all the space in my friend's unit and the common house, my place is really big."

Explaining how the building works. PHOTOS COURTESY OF CAMBRIDGE COHOUSING.

A conundrum: why are the adults, but not the children, holding their noses?

Watering the flowers by our front entrance. PHOTOS BY EDWARD A. MASON.

The youngest cohouser waters the flowers too.

Cleaning up our new mailroom.

Who gets to hold the baby today?

Common mealtime. PHOTOS COURTESY OF CAMBRIDGE COHOUSING.

Pick a partner and share your ideas.

Impromptu gathering on an East End patio. PHOTO COURTESY OF CAMBRIDGE COHOUSING.

A dad and his daughter work together. PHOTO BY EDWARD A. MASON.

Ten

Settling in, Commoning, and Complaining

As we began what was to be our first full year all together, the building still was not finished. The cooling hadn't worked in the summer and the heating wasn't working in the winter, so pipes froze. Some of the walls, ceilings, and floors between units transmitted sounds and smells from neighboring units. Workmen showed up now and again to finish this or that, but the list of work to be done grew as more construction flaws were discovered.

In February, Don, who was heading up our Community Committee, which set the time and agenda for our monthly general meetings, wondered whether we should cancel that month's meeting because all we had to talk about was the HVAC. "Personally, I think possibly having to cancel the meeting when there are clearly issues all over the place is a symptom of problems that we have as a community, and perhaps someday I'll speak my piece, but not now."

In response, Betsy did speak her piece. "I think you hit this one on the head. How can we not have anything to talk about in a meeting when we have a huge expensive issue with our HVAC system? . . . If this was a house that I owned, by myself, I would have called a halt to the obviously dysfunctional professionals we have working on this. . . . I don't feel like we have a process where a decision like this can be considered, never mind approved. I feel powerless in the face of increased utility costs, discomfort, health hazards, and time spent on the whole mess. But I think it's time to stop throwing good time after bad, and worth spending some good money. Just MHO."

Actually, we did have a process for such a decision. The DOC, sometimes jointly with the managing board (which Betsy was on), discussed changing our professionals in midstream and had consulted our lawyer to see if that was feasible or wise. Many of us felt we were in over our heads and would never get to the far shore.

While we despaired, our developers and architect busied themselves applying for prizes. An article in the Winter 1999 issue of *Conservation Matters* touted Gwen as the nation's leading "earth friendly" developer, noting that our project "had become a talking piece [that] earned recognition from professionals in the field." It had been selected "as an exemplary environmental project" by the American Institute of Architects' Committee on the Environment. The AIA also selected our project as the U.S. case study for the International Green Building Challenge. These kudos, said Bruce, were "more than ample compensation" for his difficulties with "consensual decision making." "It was like having forty-one different bosses," he grumbled.

The forty-one different bosses were grumbling, too—at our prizewinning buildings and at one another. As part of our efforts to create a communal social structure, we created a reconciliation committee, but in keeping with the personal freedom of the market, butting heads were not required to take their disagreements there. Thus its members sat by, watching helplessly as antagonisms between people grew. For example, there was the spat between Deb and Francesca over who owned Monday dinner.

Deb thought she owned it, ever since she'd put up a pizza sign-up sheet for one Monday dinner and many people signed up and enjoyed their pizza together. She did the same the next Monday and the next, until every Monday became Deb's pizza dinner. But on our first Memorial Day together, Francesca and Fran decided a barbecue/potluck supper would be a good idea and they put up a sign-up sheet. Trouble was, Memorial Day fell on a Monday and they hadn't consulted Deb.

Deb was angry and let Francesca know it. That might have been a private spat between the two of them, but Charles gave it a community-wide audience on our Listserv:

Tuesday, May 25, 1999

. . . The latest on floor three is Deb chewing Francesca out because Francesca and Fran are organizing a Memorial Day barbecue potluck. Deb chewed Francesca out for that last night claiming that she, Deb, had a proprietary jurisdiction over Monday nights and that Francesca and Fran should have cleared the Memorial Day event with her before doing it. I think that is absurd, but I also think that Deb is probably doing a goose and gander game and saying if she should have checked with IDA (read Francesca) over the couches [Deb put in the living room], then Francesca should have checked with Deb over Monday night. Actually, I guess, that F&F should have checked with the frivolity committee (read Marilyn) or the meals committee (read Joan) if they should have checked with anybody. Indeed, Deb probably should have checked with one of those committees and become a subcommittee of one of them before she took ownership of Monday night. That is getting very litigious, which I hope we will avoid. In truth, nobody owns Monday night and I guess somebody has to get that across to Deb.

Someone must have talked to Deb, because she did relinquish the Monday night pizza/potluck to the Meals committee and under its aegis kept running it until, after a while, it became a community pizza/ potluck and others also signed up to order the pizza, prepare the dining room, and clean it up, but the animosity between Francesca and Deb festered.

With hardly any rules and no structure for leadership, it did not take much for this pair of cohousers and then that pair to get into a squabble that would leave a residue of bad feelings. Sometimes plans to bring us warm community feelings would backfire. That happened when we tried to stain our fencing and our balconies ourselves during our first summer together. We had taken on the job because we were going over budget and Gwen said our fencing would cost half as much if we stained it ourselves. Some of us decided that it would be a good community-building exercise if we spent the summer like a bunch of Tom Sawyer's friends, staining our fences. We'd start with the fencing around our property and then proceed to wash and stain each other's decks and balconies.

Just as we had no rules that might have required butting heads to seek help reconciling their differences, we had no rules requiring anyone to participate in the staining or any other work that needed doing. Strong voices, especially Joan's and David's, fought every suggestion that we institute a few rules, arguing that each of us should do only what we felt like doing. So, over the summer, the fencing around our little acre and a quarter got a base coat, and by fall some of it was finished. Some decks and balconies had been washed and stained, too. But as the air was becoming brisk and the days were growing shorter, there was still much to be done and it looked as though the snows would come while a lot of bare wood was still exposed. Some of us began hiring helpers to finish our balconies, and that exposed us to the ways in which we had actually managed to achieve a bit of diversity: our differences in income, strength, and free time.

Once again, the Listserv became our forum, and Betsy was outspoken:

While many of us are deeply worried about our finances and don't want to shell out money when we can do the work ourselves, the reality seems to be that as a community we are just not into sweat equity. Cleaning, fence painting, deck staining—all seem to require paid help to get completely done and I think its wishful thinking to imagine otherwise. I hate to set up a two-tier society where some of us pay for services and others contribute their labor, but I'd hate even more to have this two-tier society and pretend we don't.

To which Ellen, a fifty-something who was our frivolity facilitator, added:

I think it is more complicated, and less ominous, than "a two-tier society where some of us pay for services and others contribute their labor." Most, if not all, of the people who sometimes pay for help also take part in the physical work, as well as other important work in the community. They simply may not have the time and/or the stamina to do as much physical work as they feel responsible for. And in the particular situation of the decks, because of the weather, we can't keep working on it indefinitely as our time and energy permit.

She went on to explain how much work she had already done:

It IS more community-building and fun to work together, and I really enjoyed the day I spent working with Axel and Jessica on my balconies and their deck. But time is getting short, and with the many decks still needing work, I didn't expect that my balconies would get finished by waiting for the community to help. . . . I sincerely hope that, after the work I've put in on the deck staining project and the garden workday, neighbors will not see me as part of some "leisure class" when they see Ed out on my balcony this weekend, finishing it up for me.

Betsy commiserated:

> Ellen—I hope your clarification about how you got your deck done gets out to all the right parties. For the record, Ellen, it really doesn't matter to me how you personally got your deck done; it just matters that we have set up an expectation that we're not meeting (that the community would provide the labor to get all decks and railings done) and now have to figure out how to address it in a way that is fair to those who have provided labor, those who have paid for help, those who have done both, and those who have done neither. In the meantime, I would really like us to look at the second paragraph of your message: It makes me feel less than happy to be in a situation where we are "not keeping track," yet people do keep track in various ways, and there is resentment against people who pay instead of work, and I wrote a long email to explain exactly what I was doing, so it wouldn't be misconstrued—and people get it wrong anyway!

In October, Ellen, Bonnie, and I went to a national cohousing conference that was held at Pioneer Valley Cohousing in Amherst, Massachusetts, and Ellen came home with an idea:

> Our ongoing discussions and tensions about paying for work versus contributing labor, assessments versus donations, etc. have reminded me of something I heard at the National Coho Conference. One community, feeling major tensions about just this kind of thing, had a meeting where people just talked about money: the circumstances and attitudes people grew up with, and the problems and feelings they were dealing with in the present. They said that even though, of course, both disparities in resources and differences in attitudes remained, it really helped to deepen understanding and alleviate tensions. What do people think about trying this?

Nothing came of Ellen's suggestion. A month later, on Wednesday, November 19, 1999, Viv entered the conversation:

I think we really need TIME to talk about some of these issues and feelings and maybe even have an impartial facilitator. IF ONLY I had been smart enough to find someone to pay to do my balcony, some of my agitation at having used up precious (and costly) vacation days would have been relieved. Of course, you can imagine my feelings now that I am hearing that that time I spent really isn't to be "counted" (by anonymous counters) as work day time. Or am I hearing that incorrectly?

All I know is that on Rosh Hashanah I did as it was suggested and cleared my balcony so it could be washed, but it never got done. (So, Nancy and I did it together with Anna's help!) I also know that I can now look at my balcony and know that it is protected from the elements, at least for this winter, and it looks pretty good. And I accomplished it all by myself!

Congratulations to me!!! And congratulations to Ellen who was resourceful and discovered a way to get help!!! And congratulations to everyone else who worked so hard on ALL the decks and balconies, a major undertaking. Let's try to celebrate our accomplishments either individually or together. There have been MANY!!! I know it's hard to do (at least for me) but I really think we need to try REALLY HARD to emphasize any and all accomplishments. Let's also try really hard to minimize the negatives. . . .

Sometimes, when we weren't struggling with the building's flaws, we did celebrate ourselves and our "team of professionals," especially Gwen, for having gotten us from our first meeting back in the fall of 1995 to our final November 1998 move-in more quickly than any other cohousing community.

How Many Cohousers
Does It Take to Change a Lightbulb

Many of us began, right after we moved in, to quietly do what needed to be done. Thus Francesca, who likes to garden and really cares about the way things look, can be seen most days in the spring, summer, and fall working on our flowering borders. Her husband, Gerard, quietly straightens up the garbage bins, though occasionally in desperation he'll send an email to the Listserv, reminding us that garbage does not go in the recycling bins. We have an excellent exercise room thanks to the efforts of a small group who just got to work equipping it and managing to get equipment contributed, all without much fanfare.

But if no one assumes responsibility for something, we can spend months of meetings and messages on our Listserv trying to solve a very small problem. Take changing lightbulbs, for example. No joke. On Saturday, September 19, 1998, shortly after he moved in to his town house in the West End, Frank noticed a problem and sent out a note on our Listserv: "When you enter the [East] End basement you can turn on the light in the downstairs area at the top of the stairs. But if someone turns it off upstairs you cannot turn it on downstairs. It becomes dangerously dark even in the day. Does the house committee deal with this electrical snafu?? There should be a two-way switch controlled both from up and downstairs."

Jon, one of our three master techies, an East Ender who had moved in at the beginning of February 1998, had already dealt with the problem: "For the time being, we're using the following protocol: Use the upstairs switch ONLY! Please do not use the downstairs switch—leave it in the ON position! Why?"

As Jon is wont to do, he added a long explanation. Then Ellen added some history: "At our first informational meeting with Bruce and Mark in the EE basement, I asked about the light switches. Bruce said he thought the plans called for a switch just inside the basement door from the stairwell, which could control the basement and stairwell lights separately. I don't know if that ever got onto a list. While we're on the subject of lights, does anyone know why all the lights are out on the EE 2d floor hallway? Has anyone been contacted to fix it?"

To which, Florence, who was always quick to suggest a simple and obvious solution, asked, "Has anyone tried putting in a new bulb?"

Almost a year later, on Monday, August 30, 1999, someone sent out another email: "Subject: So many bulbs, not enough light. Does anyone know what is going on about the lights? I can't seem to turn on the lights in the Common-house spine when it is dark, but they were on a couple of nights ago."

On and on it went, and we were not alone. The wags on the national Listserv were having a good time asking how many cohousers it takes to change a lightbulb. My contribution went something like this:

> Thousands: There's the meeting to come to consensus that the bulb has indeed burned out and it is not faulty wiring. There's the meeting to come to consensus that we have too many lights and that one bulb should be left burned out. There's the meeting to revisit that consensus when someone trips in the darkened hallway. There's the meeting to come to consensus that if another bulb burns out we should use energy-saving bulbs. There's the meeting to come to consensus that we need a volunteer to find the best place to buy the energy-saving bulbs. There's the meeting to come to consensus that the money should come from the general budget. And so on.

In our case, there finally was a meeting to accept Kit's offer when he became so fed up with a year of talk and no action that he decided to come to the rescue. The minutes of the managing board, November 30, 1999, note that "Kit J. has volunteered to be the Coho lighting 'czar.' He will replace bulbs, as they are needed. In so doing he will be balancing lighting needs, energy efficiency and appearance. Waverly (the managing company) will be requested to change any hard to reach bulbs."

The announcement was repeated at the next general meeting and we all applauded. Kit graciously demurred, saying he needed no thanks for just doing his part. But that was not the end of it. The very next day, Charles sent the following email: "That's really great. Kit should check out floor 2. We kept hearing a light bulb crew would be around imminently, but nothing happened. Long burning compact fluorescents might be best there, no? Pretty dark hallways when the bulbs are out (no windows at all there)."

I guess Kit obeyed Charles's demand and did what he could to keep us in the light for several years, but on September 12, 2004, Kit announced his resignation at the general meeting: "I can steer you to bulbs, a ladder, and the combination to our paint room. I resign lights duty." Fortunately, by that time a new managing board had decided to switch managing companies, and ever since we've paid for and enjoyed the services of a Cadillac managing company and they keep the lights on (or off), showing how much simpler it can be just to pay someone to do some things. Sometimes markets can be more efficient than commons.

As we settled in, our way of life took shape. Issues with the buildings popped up from day to day and year to year as this or that part broke down and had to be repaired or replaced. But slowly we did get the buildings to work, so that after a decade or so, maintenance and repairs became the responsibility of the managing board and the rest of us could go about our lives.

We were getting to know each other. Friendships were developing as some of us invited others to dinner, and our meals program developed into a regular pattern of a Monday night pizza/potluck, a Wednesday or Thursday dinner, and something over the weekend—a brunch on Sunday or a dinner or potluck supper on Saturday or Sunday. As everything depended on volunteer energies, the issues that were addressed depended partly on need—you couldn't ignore an HVAC system that wasn't working—and partly on who was willing to do the work—that's how we have our garden, our exercise room, and our meals. Some of us continued to live at Cambridge Cohousing as we might have lived in any condominium, paying our fees and minding only our own business—never showing up at meals or meetings and giving voice only when something displeased us. Most of us participated at least a little bit, and some of us gave a lot. As Michael noted, "We, like all organizations, followed the Pareto principle: 20% of the input was responsible for 80% of the results, or, in our case, 20% of us did 80% of the work."

In 2000, we gave up trying to get everyone to adopt and take care of a room or area in our common house. We hired a cleaning company, and in 2001, under Francesca's direction, the workers began cleaning the stairs and floor landings in the common house. In 2002, an engineer declared our newly washed and stained balconies unsafe, and we tore them down, put up new ones, and got our contractor to contribute something, but not much, to the cost. In 2003, we noted that air passed quite freely from one unit to the next, so we invoked the famous dictum "Your freedom ends where my nose begins" and passed a no-smoking policy. By 2004, I was feeling enough at home at Cambridge Cohousing that I had stopped escaping for the holidays.

A New Year's to Remember

Kate made New Year's Eve 2005 very special. New Year's Eve had usually been a simple affair at Cambridge Cohousing. Whoever had nothing better to do would gather by the fire at about nine or ten with some fancy hors d'oeuvres and desserts. In 2005, however, at the December general meeting, Kate announced with her "I'm so excited, I could die" smile that she was organizing New Year's Eve and it would be a fancy dress-up, potluck dinner that would start at seven. By the Chanukah party, though, no one had signed up and New Year's Eve was only two days off, Chanukah being very late that year.

Francesca, who was sitting across from me, wondered what to do. I said, "Well, seven o'clock is too early for New Year's Eve; we should do what we always do and not start until nine or ten." Giggling that neither of us was brave enough to speak to Kate alone, we agreed to go together to talk to her to see if she would be willing to have her dinner start a bit later. But on Friday, just as I was preparing to call Francesca, she called me to say that Isabel and John had signed up for a bûche de Noël (which I learned was a traditional holiday cake shaped like a log and studded with mushrooms made from chocolate frosting and lots of whipped cream) and Jim and Lyn were bringing chicken Florentine—the dinner was on.

All day, snow threatened. It moved eastward from the Mississippi to the Great Lakes, then through the Berkshires, and finally to Cambridge. By two in the afternoon, it had covered my skylights, bringing with it a false dusk. As I pulled the drapes, I noticed the rooftops of neighboring houses, their wet edges outlined shiny black beneath a thickening white blanket. Snowflakes sparkled in the light along the glade and the trunks and branches of trees were black beneath their growing white cover. It was quiet and beautiful and I thought how nice it was not to have to go out.

It would be my seventh New Year's at Cambridge Cohousing, but only the second that I'd risked extreme loneliness to spend it with my fellow cohousers. At seven o'clock, I rang for the elevator, dressed as close to the nines as I cared to be, a black velvet square-cut blouse above flowing black pants, the pearls Dick had given me topping it off. The elevator slowed for a stop on the third floor, revealing Sybil and Roland, a pleasant surprise. Earlier, Sybil had said they might only pop in but probably wouldn't come for dinner. Now there they were with their basket filled with dishes and a bowl with their contribution to the potluck offerings. My basket held a

Wedgwood plate with smoked salmon; a glistening silver butter knife stabbed a ball of cream cheese at its center.

The living room wasn't exactly hopping, but the fire was blazing and Viv had put a plate overflowing with shrimp on the coffee table. "I couldn't decide whether to buy one pound or two at Trader Joe's," she said, "so I bought two."

Roland and I took our baskets into the dining room. It was transformed. The lights were dimmed and Kate had pushed tables together to make a large square table with room for five or six diners on each side. Instead of the red plastic tablecloths, Kate had put out our blue-and-white-checkered cotton ones, but over them in the center, she had spread a white lace cloth. Three large crystal candelabra with foot-tall candles sparkled in the center. Roland asked where we should sit, and Kate, calling from the kitchen, said, "Anywhere, just as long as you leave a place for me by the kitchen."

The living room began to fill. Ted and Barbara came, he with his thermos-size canister of oxygen, which was now his constant companion. Everybody made a fuss to find a place for him away from the fire and candles. Then Alex emerged from the kitchen, all dressed up in a suit and tie. "Do you often dress up in a suit and tie?" someone asked while the rest of us admired his getup. "No, only for funerals and weddings, and now because Kate said we should all dress up." "Oh no, you didn't have to for me," said Kate, laughing; then she smiled at me and said I looked beautiful. "Is that a dress?" she asked. "No, just some old bell bottoms that have come back into fashion," I replied. "I'm going to date myself," said Roland, "but I can remember when everybody went to work in a suit and tie." We all agreed it was better to get dressed up only occasionally.

Basil and Naomi arrived. Naomi's long gray hair was fashioned in a bun on the top of her head and she was wearing something handmade and folksy. Basil, slight and always smiling through his thick glasses, said they were sorry to be late, but their grandkids just left and they could barely stand. Francesca entered next, looking gaunt but striking in a red jacket and no hat on her chemo-balded, beautifully round head. Gerard was wearing a fancy vest.

With a clapping of hands, Kate announced dinner. We each took a seat at the huge table. I sat catty-corner to Roland, who had Sybil to his left, with Kate a couple of seats farther down on that side. Hands were raised for silence and Kate announced the menu, as she had earlier in an email that promised "fancy mashed potatoes with a very Swedish name" from Alex, whose next email said, "The potatoes are not mashed. The potatoes & I are of the opinion that mashing is a terrible fate for a potato. :-) Sliced very thin into match-sticks and baked with cream and butter and breadcrumbs in a very light & airy dish is much better, flavored with anchovies and sau-téed onions. The name of the dish is Jansson's Temptation, and you have to assume that it's got to be pretty good if a Swede was tempted by it when it involved no alcohol."

Once again Kate stumbled on her description of the potatoes and once again Alex described the dish. Then all of us took our plates to the large mahogany table in the center of the room. That table had been my mother's pride, my major contribution to Fran-cesca's furnishing our common house with stuff that wouldn't fit in our units. There was a lamb roast, and a turkey roast that Kate contributed, guaranteeing that no matter what others did or didn't bring, this would be a festive dinner. Next to the roasts were Alex's potatoes, laid out in a large glass roasting pan. Sonia had brought a large bowl of rice, and at the other end of the table was a cranberry and orange salad that Marge had made. Buttered green beans shin-ing in their large white bowl came from Bob and Colette, and there was a large serving dish of chicken Florentine from Jim and Lyn. A surprise was a bowl filled with Swedish meatballs, alongside it a bowl of sauce that Ned, who was one of the men in the special-needs unit, had brought. Someone must have bought it for him at the Ikea store that had just opened in Stoughton. Ned loved to eat and often appeared at meals without the others from his unit.

The table was so large, you could only talk to whomever was next to you. Francesca, who was to my right, was talking to Sybil, who was to her right. Gerard was across the table at Carol's right. I'd never seen Gerard and Francesca sitting so far apart. Naomi's Roland was clear across the table. Once at dinner, I'd told Roland how nice I thought it was that he and Naomi didn't always sit together. He said, "Oh, we see enough of each other." I think if Dick had still been alive, we would have been sitting apart, too. At big parties, we always separated. That way, we'd have stories to tell each other when we got home. Though we might have wanted to sit together on New Year's Eve.

In the afternoon, I had called my old friend Joan to wish her a happy New Year. She had just fallen and hurt her leg. A friend had driven her home, but she didn't know if she would be able to get upstairs to her bed. We talked till our ears hurt, catching up on our children, joking about the latest horror from Bush, and wondering whether he had finally lost enough support to lose some congressional seats in the 2006 election, but doubting that he had or that it would make any difference, given the way they'd jimmied the ballots in Florida and Ohio when it looked as though they might be losing. When Joan asked how cohousing was working, I said that it was getting better and better—every time someone moved out, someone better moved in. She sounded a little wistful. Joan's not a complainer, always sounding as cheerful as she can, but she did, for the first time since I've known her, talk about being alone and lonely.

Joan was the first to be widowed. I remember the day. Someone called us—I think it was Jane—and we went right over. The police officer had called Stew because he was her minister, and the officer thought it would be better if Stew told Joan about the accident.

Wilton, Connecticut, in those days was that kind of community. It was so small that it didn't have its own police department. Instead, we had a state trooper who pretty much knew everybody in town. Not that everybody knew everybody else; it wasn't that small or stable, but there were probably only two degrees of separation between any of us: If you didn't know somebody, you probably did know someone who did—except for the corporation managers, that is, who were moving in and out again at a two-year clip. They were changing everything, and Wilton today is not the same kind of town it was then. For one thing, it's much more upscale.

I thought about moving back to Wilton when Dick died, but by then, most of our friends had moved out. Stew and Jane were the first to go when he got a call from a church in Texas. Then Joan bought a co-op in New York City around the same time she inherited a wonderful summer house near Lake Waramaug, in Connecticut. She was there now, alone this New Year's Eve.

I was pleased not to be alone. Not that cohousing can take the place of a spouse. Sometimes it's even harder when you're single in cohousing. For instance, there are things couples do where they don't invite singles. Like the good-bye dinner Fran and Richard staged for the Loos a few years ago. There they all were having a fine old time, laughing and eating right under my window, with the smoke and aroma wafting through my open slider, so I couldn't have missed it if I'd tried. Kate said at some meeting that she was lonely here, and Barbara said she was surprised to hear that. "I don't feel lonely here," Barbara said. I pointed out that Barbara was married and said I wasn't at all surprised that Kate was lonely here, as this was a hard place for singles.

Now and then at meetings, I had tried to bring up the difficulties singles faced, but I had been talked down every time. Barbara said she didn't feel there was a problem, that it wasn't any worse here than any other place for singles. If people expected cohousing to be an answer to their loneliness, they had unreasonable expectations. That brought to my mind something Peter had said some years back: "It's only cohousing," a phrase which comes back to mind whenever I reflect on my loneliness here. No question about it, I'd rather be having New Year's Eve dinner here than being all alone as Joan was that evening. Still, it was only cohousing. I wouldn't be reviewing all our New Year's Eves together with Dick.

Private Property Meets the Commons . . . Again!

Through all those years, at about the rate of one move a year, some of our founders moved away and were replaced by newcomers. The turnover usually occurred with little fanfare, but in 2005, a series of moves highlighted an issue where once again private property edged up to our commons. This time, the problem was in the storage room in the common house. Once again, the East End was spared the difficulties. All their town houses had basements; only the six units in the stacked flats shared a storage room.

The Common-House and West End were a different story. There the garage precluded basements in all but three of the town houses, and the twenty-seven units in the common house, stacked flats, and town houses without a basement had to share one storage room. Now and again, someone would complain. For example, this comment from the minutes of the managing board meeting of January 8, 2001:

> The Sarah move-in has naturally precipitated into stark awareness the fact that [the storage room is] in chaos. Two members present at this meeting volunteered that their "stuff" was clearly stored in other's spaces. Sarah needs and deserves her fair share of storage space. She is correct in requesting it. Bill may be forced to move other people's stuff out of his (presently theoretical) space. This will compound the general problem. This is a community wide problem (except for town houses with basements) and it remains to be solved.

The minutes in August show that nothing had been solved: "There are serious problems of boundary creep as residents store into their neighbors' space. . . . Hopefully, involved parties can settle among themselves." That went on for four more years, until 2006, when Maria and Alan's move to Cambridge Cohousing forced us into a serious round of storage-space negotiations. Explaining their surprising new role to me, Maria, a woman as delicate in her ways as she was in appearance, said, "I don't know why, but we just expected to have some space; maybe because we had been shown the storage on one of the tours, but we just knew that everybody had some storage space. The Realtor may have shown the storage room to us, but she didn't know the exact space. Then on moving day, we came down there and, oops, no space."

"What about Caroline's space?" I asked. Maria and Alan had bought Caroline's town house when she moved to California.

"I guess Caroline had never used her space," Maria said. "She was a single woman and probably was able to store everything in the town house. Someone told us to talk to Peter about it. I think Perter managed to talk to the people who had put their stuff in our space and eventually got them to clean up, but meanwhile our stuff had to sit in the hall for weeks. It bothered me that my stuff was just sitting out there. And it must have been bothering other people, too."

I was surprised when Maria said that she thought she was shown the storage room on a tour. I'm the one who usually does the tours at CCH, and though I always take people down to the basement, I hardly ever take my storage room key with me. It's fun to show off the basement, even though at one point (until IDA got around to painting it) its walls were a dingy, much smudged white. There's our exercise room with its treadmills, stationary bicycles, and universal weight machine, and there's the former teen room with the self-portraits painted by the six kids who were teens when we moved in. I like to proudly open the door to the garage and say, "There are more Priuses here than in any other place except on a Toyota sales lot." And I can usually make a point about cohousing when I show the laundry room with its shelves full of detergents and say that's one thing we've never gotten around to co-ing. Usually someone asks why not and I opine that it's probably because no one has taken the time to organize it. In a commons, someone has to take the lead when something needs to be done.

Opening the door to the rec room always gets an appreciative "ooh"—it is brightly painted in Crayola primaries and has a pool table and in one corner a small stage and cubbies full of dress-up clothes. Except for the wall with photos documenting our genesis, from signing our LLP agreement in September 1996 until our dedication celebration in November 1998, that's about it for the basement. I never do more than point down the gray passageway across from the stairs, saying that's where the storage room and mechanical room are. Once someone wanted to see the storage room. She had heard that there is never enough storage in cohousing. She was probably right. One of the arguments in favor of cohousing is that people living in a cohousing community, because they share so much in common, don't need as much storage space or anything else.

For example, making the case for cohousing, Peter Lazar, who later became president of the national cohousing organization, wrote:

> The cohousing "common house," which contains guest rooms, home offices and other common amenities, further promotes affordability because the individual homes don't need as many rooms and can thereby be smaller. When our family moved from a 2400 sq. ft. house to a 1800 sq. ft. house in a cohousing community, we expected it to be a sacrifice. We discovered, though, that 1800 sq. ft. almost seems too large for my family of four. Because we share large items (such as a lawnmower and tools)

with neighbors, we don't need as much storage space. We also don't need such a large living or dining room because we can entertain many guests in our beautiful common house (Lazar 2006).

At Cambridge Cohousing, our architect probably took that kind of talk much too seriously, especially when it came to storage. Not long after Maria and Alan's move, Sophie and Cora moved into Fran and Richard's common house unit, and when they went to put their stuff in the storage room, same story. They created a small crisis by not storing their stuff in the basement corridor, as Maria and Alan had done, but instead putting it in the second-floor hall, where it was hard to ignore. That got Joan, Sophie's mother, into the act, and when Joan gets into the act, something happens. It may not be exactly what everybody wants to see happen, but in one way or another there will be a shift from the usual catch-as-catch-can attitude, putting your stuff wherever it will fit, to ORDER!

So it happened that the fall of 2006 and much of 2007 became the year to revisit our storage arrangements. Not that a lot of other things didn't happen, as well: We bought and put up a huge ice-skating rink on the front lawn, we painted the basement, Ellen was born, and we set up a new and improved security plan for the West End and common house. Interspersed with all that, and a lot more, so many hours were spent working out a storage plan we could all agree on that, had we paid for those hours at our normal rates of pay, we might have been able to use the funds to construct a nice big building just for storage.

Not that we hadn't already spent many hours developing a plan for storage. In those heady days, when after more than a year of delays we were finally moving in, many plans for divvying up the storage room were presented and discussed. The problem was that none was fully implemented. Squatter's stuff was in the space that belonged to Maria and Alan's town house and Sophie's common house unit because, during the first round of negotiations about storage space, many of the groups Peter had dubbed "co-storage communities" never did get around to assigning particular spaces to each unit.

When our fourth-floor denizens met to find a way to satisfy everyone, I won the everlasting affection of Sally, who shared a one-bedroom unit with Bert, and, I hoped, the not so long-lasting enmity of Barbara in her four-bedroom unit, by opening the meeting with the suggestion that we still had to decide on the principle of distribution our floor would choose. Barbara said we had already decided: that it would be proportional to the size of our units. I said no, that we were still free to choose whether it would be, as Barbara wished, proportional to our unit size—in other words, to the richest goes the most, a formula to warm the heart of any free-enterprise proponent—or, what might seem equally reasonable, especially to a commoner, that we might decide that the smallest units should have the most storage space because those in smaller units had less room in their units to store things. After much talk, during which Peter's calculations received nary a word, our floor came to consensus on equality: We'd each get the same amount of storage space.

That solved one part of the problem. We had yet to decide how much space each of us would get in the former laundry room on our floor and how much in the basement storage room. Once more, we decided on equality. That meant we had to divvy up our allotment in the basement storage room and the fifty-four square feet in what was a laundry room in the plans. First, we had to accomplish the second item on Peter's list, which was to "subtract the necessary circulation from the total square footage." In the fourth-floor former laundry room, we began by deducting nine feet from the fifty-four so that the three-foot door could swing open. That left forty-five feet, or nine square feet for each of us. Barbara and Ted had a four-by-two-foot steel cabinet that they wanted to put in the old laundry room. It had doors on either side that swung out two feet. No amount of drawings and talk could convince Barbara that if nobody could put anything in the two feet in front of her cabinet, she and Ted were effectively taking up not only the eight square feet their cabinet stood upon but also the eight square feet in front of their cabinet that the doors swung into. That added up to sixteen square feet, about one-third of the available space, rather than the one-fifth to which they were entitled. To compromise, I agreed that half my space would be the air space above their cabinet, where I could put a mover's cardboard wardrobe to store out-of-season clothes.

Ellen said she had twelve sets of tall shelves that anybody could have. Bert put one of them next to Ted and Barbara's cabinet. In true cohousing spirit, Viv, Barbara, and I decided to share a vacuum cleaner, which we stored in the space in front of Barbara and Ted's cabinet. We also stored other shared cleaning equipment behind the door. Then a ladder appeared, which was very useful in allowing me to get to my upper-level wardrobe. And somehow, just as mysteriously, three sets of shelves just like Bert's appeared for Viv, Donna, and me. They stood against the two other walls. Then one day, a twin-size mattress showed up in front of Bert and Anastasia's shelves. When others complained, Anastasia slipped into her mad-Russian act, the one she adopted when Kate complained of the noise from her air conditioner.

Threatened with the loss of it, Anastasia had gone out on her balcony and screamed, "I cannot stand it; I jump. In Russia, it not so hot, too humid here." About the mattress, she breathlessly declaimed, "My mother, she all I have, she die six months ago, I cannot put her in basement; I die, too."

The mattress smelled bad; it not only made the whole room smell bad but, over time, it would make everything in the room smell bad. Viv agreed with me; she said she wouldn't put anything in there till the mattress was out, and it looked for a while as though Bert and Anastasia had found a way to get the whole former laundry room to themselves. I certainly wasn't going to say anything to Anastasia about her dead mother's mattress. But somebody must have, because a few weeks after it appeared, the mattress disappeared. Viv and

Donna were pretty silent about being reduced from nine to three square feet, but during the years between the first and second storage negotiations, Barbara complained volubly and often about the suitcases, air filters, vacuum cleaner, and other stuff that migrated to the space in front of her cabinet.

When Peter had instructed us in the newsletter to "reallocate individual chunks proportionate to the by-right numbers and distribute storage rights to its members: by area, volume, or by need," he added, "hopefully not by squatter's rights, name calling, hair pulling, etc." As far as I know, we never did regress to name-calling or hair pulling, but as the stuff in front of Barbara and Ted's cabinet and Maria and Alan's moving-day surprise demonstrate, stuff abhors a vacuum. Whatever space was left vacant was quickly filled with squatter's stuff. One reason was that we never did accomplish Peter's third assignment: "shelves/partitions should be constructed either by an outside contractor or by a work team of the House Committee." "This" he claimed, "is the way to live together in harmony."

Almost a decade later, under the guidance of Peter and Joan, we renegotiated the space each unit would be allowed, we invested in steel shelving, we took everything out of the storage room and reassembled it, assigning a space to each unit, and to this day we use only our own spaces, even leaving unused spaces empty. Commoners who are well managed do live in harmony.

Eleven

A Time to Weep
and a Time to Cheer

Years ago, a visitor from a cohousing community in Iceland, who had visited the community in Denmark that had given birth to the cohousing movement, told us that the most important time to be living in cohousing was at a sad time, during a divorce or when a death occurred. When I heard that, I thought, Yes, it would have been better to be living in a cohousing community when Dick died. I would not have been so alone then, and my neighbors in Cambridge Cohousing would have known Dick and shared my loss. But our visitor from Iceland was only half right. It is just as important to be living in community during times of celebration. In fact, it may be harder to cheer alone than it is to grieve alone.

Two thousand and eight was a year for both cheering and grieving. In late May, after about a month of wondering why my stomach was so bloated, I went for my annual physical and told my doctor I was afraid I might have cancer. She confirmed my fear, and sent me for an ultrasound. When I got home, I was thinking about whom I would tell and how, when there was Francesca, walking down the stairs as I was walking up. She had just come back from some trip, but I wasn't thinking about that. I didn't even greet her; I just blurted out, "You're the first one I see, so I might as well tell you." And I did.

Francesca was an experienced guide: She had been diagnosed with ovarian cancer three years earlier and had become a regular volunteer at Boston's Dana-Farber Cancer Institute. She plied me with information, loaning me books and pamphlets to read, and she visited doctors with me. When I became dissatisfied with the treatment I was receiving at another Boston hospital, she talked her oncologist at Dana-Farber into taking me on. My sister thought I should hire a nurse for my return from the hospital, but I thought that was a crazy idea. She just didn't get it about cohousing. I had to explain that Francesca had offered to stay with me and that if I needed anything, all I had to do was ask and someone would get it for me. I explained some of what we had done for each other: that there was a sign-up now for Kate, so that there would be someone to drive her home from the hospital and someone to take dinner to her whenever she had to go for chemo; that I had taken Francesca to acupuncture while she was having chemo; that when Viv broke her arm in Italy and called to have someone pick her up at the airport and I couldn't because I was in Connecticut, teaching that day, I put a notice on our Listserv and Axel went to get her.

I had ovarian cancer, but I was one of the lucky ones. Although the tumor was huge—somewhere between a grapefruit and a volleyball—it was still just stage 1A; all those nasty cells were still completely contained in the tumor; they had not metastasized. Very unusual. Because it is so difficult to detect early on, only about 10 percent of ovarian cancer victims are diagnosed before the cancer metastasizes. Fortunately, I was one of the 10 percent, and fortunately, Francesca was there to guide me.

How different it would have been without CCH. Without CCH, I probably would not even have known Francesca. Our paths were not likely to have crossed. Many fellow cohousers feel that we have failed in our diversity goals, but we are more diverse than most neighborhoods, which usually are composed of people of the same income level, the same race and ethnicity, and often even the same age. Friendship groups often form at school or work or at places of worship and in neighborhoods. Francesca is an army brat, a Catholic, about ten years younger than I am. We might have sat side by side at a concert or bumped into each other on the street, but without cohousing, it's unlikely we would have gotten to know each other and become friends.

Because I live in Cambridge Cohousing, I know Francesca and many other people with different kinds of life experiences, people who will immediately lend their knowledge and strength to get me through any kind of problem I may face. It gives a different slant to diversity. Often what separates people are not differences in backgrounds, but differences in values and politics, and cohousers are likely to discuss and share values and politics.

An Election to Remember

Those shared values and beliefs became clear on November 4, 2008, the day Obama was elected president. As it happened, Election Day was the same day as the regular meeting of the CCH Community Life committee. I was its facilitator. As facilitator, I might have tried to reschedule the meeting, but that would have taken a week of trying to get everyone to agree on a new date. Instead, I just put together a short agenda, hoping the meeting would end before the returns started coming in.

As we began, Bert was setting up the big screen in our living room. But soon after we started, bearers of announcements that this state and then that one had turned blue for Obama disrupted our deliberations. By eight-thirty, our meeting was a shambles. No one, including me, could concentrate on the business at hand. We adjourned and all went into the living room to wait and wait and wait for McCain's resignation speech. At eleven, when the polls closed in California, McCain came on. It was, we agreed, a gracious speech. While Gerard got out the glasses, I took the elevator up to my unit on the fourth floor, where I had been chilling some bubbly. He popped the corks and we waited for Obama to get to Grant Park in Chicago and deliver his victory speech.

The next morning, on Cohousing-L, the national cohousing Listserv, Craig, who was the executive secretary of Coho/US, the national cohousing organization, posted a message describing the celebration at his community, Songaia, in the Seattle area. At Songaia, which has community dinners almost every night of the week, they listened to returns on NPR during dinner. Later, about ten community members set up an impromptu broadcast-watching party in the common house. Craig went home to do some work, but gave up shortly after McCain's concession speech, when one of the community's adolescent boys stopped by to invite Craig and his wife over for a champagne celebration in the common house. Once there, they realized that Fred, who had ALS, wasn't with them, and the party moved to Fred and Nancy's living room, where there were "lots of jokes and excitement as toasts began, considering the future of our country—with much hope about the environment, health care, education, employment, participatory democracy, and possibly even a future world of peace."

In response to Craig's subject line: "Did your community celebrate last night?" Karen wrote from her Arboretum Cohousing Community in Madison, Wisconsin; Larry reported celebrations from Oak Creek Commons, in Paso Robles, California; and Robert chimed in from Eno Commons Cohousing in Durham, North Carolina. But for some, all that cheering was too much. At about noon on Wednesday, the soul-searching began. Ann, from Tacoma Village Cohousing in Washington, D.C., wrote a long message, asking whether there was room for conservatives in cohousing. She said:

> [T]he reason I got involved in cohousing is that I immediately saw this social structure as one road to peace in the world. (If we can figure out how to live together in small communities maybe we can tackle the Middle East.) So I'm always looking for mutuality, inclusivity and connection in cohousing. . . . I know there ARE some conservative folks in—out there somewhere —but I wonder how welcome we make them feel when it looks as if there is "A" kind of political leaning? For instance . . . the question posed in this thread wasn't: What did your community do on election night? But rather: Did your community CELEBRATE last night? (emphasis mine) . . . Ok. You can now start throwing bricks and tomatoes at me!:-)

There were no bricks. Instead, Craig replied with a mea culpa: "Great point and I wish I had been more inclusive in my title."

Still, there were holdouts for joy. David, at JP Cohousing in Boston, defended Craig, concluding his post by saying:

> As far as Craig's original post, I'm fine with it, including the "Did your community celebrate last night?" subject header. I take it that he was expressing his own and likely his community's feelings, and asking whether other communities were doing the same. If a McCain supporter or a more conservative community wishes to check in with a posting requesting "Was your community in mourning last week?" they are free to post this. I presume Craig was posting personally and not as a Cohousing/USA official. In the rather distant past I might have been concerned about excluding conservatives. But with our recent experience with conservatism it is diametrically opposed to the values that are a part of cohousing. I wouldn't find it comfortable to be a part of a community in which people were unconcerned about global warming, believed

> saving embryos is more important than doing research to save the
> lives and health of living people, did not think it was a basic right
> to have medical care, believed low taxes are more important than
> education, were opposed to equal rights for gays and lesbians,
> etc. As long as the Republican party espouses values so completely
> antithetical to mine, I am not looking for political diversity.

Moving from the partisan to the analytical, Tim Mensch, who signed off saying that he is "no longer living in cohousing, and instead trying out superbia," said:

> I think that the "conservative/liberal" label makes the question too
> simplistic. People are complicated. . . . I do believe that people in
> cohousing (at least cohousing that works in the ways I've imag-
> ined and experienced it) need to prefer what George Lakoff calls
> the "Nurturing Parent" frame of thinking. Anyone who wants to
> understand why Democrats were failing for so long, or rather why
> the Republicans were succeeding, should read his book, "Don't
> Think of an Elephant." It's seriously eye-opening. In brief, Lakoff
> believes that the two "frames" that people can see the world
> from are the "Strict Father" frame, where a moral leader that you
> follow without questioning is important, and people who don't
> should be punished (think Arnold Schwarzenegger), versus the
> "Nurturing Parent" frame, where the parents (or the government)
> tries to guide and help their children (or the citizens) and protect
> them from harm.

Mensch went on to summarize Lakoff's theory. It can probably be extended to support for the commons on the one hand and support for enclosures on the other: Those who are more comfortable with the nurturing parent frame and don't like to be told what to do, do well in cohousing, support commons, are good commoners, and tend to be Democrats and progressives. Those who are more comfortable with the strict father frame want to lead or be led, are not attracted to cohousing, support enclosures, are good exchangers, and tend to be Republicans and conservatives.

At about that point, Yisreala wrote, "I am sorry . . . Can someone tell me how to unsubscribe from this list? Thanks." But Diane, from JP Cohousing, supported Tim Mensch:

> I think this pretty much nails it. The only thing I was going to add is that cooperation strikes me as more of a liberal (or "Nurturing Parent") value, whereas living in your own house that you manage independently strikes me as more of a conservative (or "Strict Father") value. I have given tours of JP cohousing to some from the "Strict Father" point of view, and they are very skeptical of how the whole cooperation thing works out. To my way of thinking this conversation is an important one to have on Cohousing-L because it helps clarify what we mean by "diversity." As Rob Sandelin pointed out many times, major conflicts in the consensus process usually revolve around conflicting values. Therefore, it makes sense to examine the underlying assumptions about "diversity" and ask ourselves what do we mean by this term? Should we encourage people with a value that differs from one of the fundamental concepts of cohousing ("cooperation") to live in this kind of a housing situation?

Cohousers seem to be on the horns of a dilemma. They want to be open and welcoming to all people, no matter their race, their religion, their sexual orientation, their family type, their age, or their politics. Yet for all its openness, cohousing does not have as broad a racial, religious, or political attraction as its members would like. From the two surveys that the Cohousing Research Network conducted in 2010 and 2016, we know the following:

- Cohousing does not have a broad geographical reach. Most cohousing communities are on either coast or are in or near major university towns.

- In 2008, all but a handful (about seven) of cohousing communities were in blue states.

- There are fewer adults under forty and more over forty living in cohousing.

- Compared to the rest of the U.S. population, a lower ratio of cohousers are either living alone or in households with children.

- Compared to the rest of the U.S. population, there are many fewer poor cohousers. Cohousers tend to be clustered in the middle range, with yearly incomes from $50,000 to $100,000.

- About 70 percent of adults in cohousing are female; over 90 percent are white.

- Whereas over 70 percent of the total U.S. population was Christian in 2010, only 27 percent of cohousers were Christian and almost half of them were Unitarian Universalist. Thirty-eight percent of cohousers are agnostic or atheist, compared to 7 percent in the rest of the U.S. population.

- The greatest difference between cohousers and the rest of the U.S. population was in terms of education, with over 60 percent of cohousers holding a graduate or professional degree and less than 5 percent having less than a bachelor's degree.

Dragon at head of the parade for the Cambridge Commons 20th anniversary
celebration. PHOTOS COURTESY OF CAMBRIDGE COMMONS.

Common house circle dance at the 20th anniversary celebration, 2018.

Enjoying dinner on the patio outside our dining room.

Solar festival feast. PHOTOS COURTESY OF CAMBRIDGE COMMONS.

Badminton on the Pretty Great Lawn. PHOTOS COURTESY OF CAMBRIDGE COMMONS.

Day of the Dead event in the common house, 2019.

Setting up a skating rink, Dec 26, 2018.

View down West End sidewalk. PHOTOS COURTESY OF CAMBRIDGE COMMONS.

Presentation at the 20th anniversary celebration.

East End veggie
garden July, 2018.
PHOTOS COURTESY OF
CAMBRIDGE COMMONS.

Play structure on the
Pretty Great Lawn

Historic agenda from 1996 planning meeting, on display at the 20th anniversary celebration.

A common meal buffet table.

20th anniversary celebration cake, 2018. PHOTOS COURTESY OF CAMBRIDGE COMMONS.

Twelve

A Renaissance
and a Pandemic

Perhaps if we had taken more time to find a site, build our infrastructure, sell our old homes, and move into our new ones, we would have thought more about the community we were trying to build. Many other cohousing communities use the longer time it takes them to build their physical structures to work out agreements among their members: rules about participation that everyone would be expected to follow, including the expectation that members would attend some meetings, give some specified time and effort to the group, bring difficulties with other members to a mediator to work out, and join with the community on a yearly retreat. Hardly any cohousing community has turned such expectations into requirements, with a system to check up on each other or a way to deal with freeloaders, but many developed more effective means of commanding participation than we did.

Our vision statement did have a few words about working together:

> We share a commitment to the idea that cooperating in the en
> deavors of daily life brings the pleasures of sociability, greater

> economy of resources and effort in daily tasks, the warmth of an
> extended family and the probability of a rich variety of friend-
> ships. . . . We want to share and interact with each other through
> social activities, celebrations and practical tasks, such as cooking,
> dining, childcare, maintenance and through other shared work
> and problem solving.

However, except when we had to decide whether there would be private gardens, we hardly ever referred to our vision statement. It was
as if our nation's Founding Fathers, having written their Declaration
of Independence, had left it to everybody to happily donate their
time, money, and lives to the glorious enterprise; no constitutional
convention, no Constitution, no means of enforcement—just a Pan-
glossian assumption of goodwill. In our case, there was goodwill,
and a lot of good work. Some of us worked longer and harder for
Cambridge Cohousing than we worked at our paid jobs. But when
things went wrong, others among us sent complaints to our Listserv,
as if some full-time superintendent or manager were being paid to
make it all work.

This was definitely not Ann Riophe's endless summer camp nor
my artists' colony. For one thing, the greatest difference between the
commons we called Cambridge Cohousing and a summer camp, artists' colony, school, corporation, corner grocery store, or symphony
orchestra is that these other organizations have directors, bosses,
managers, owners, conductors—leaders of one sort or another who
organize them and have the authority and power to demand and receive compliance. I was in favor of a leaderless community, and not
until one evening in 2003 did I realize why it wasn't working.

I was enjoying a short visit for alumni at Blue Mountain Center, the writer's and artist's colony in the Adirondacks where Dick
and I had enjoyed several residencies. We were sitting or standing
around the fire that Ben, the director, had built and were chatting about the terrible state the world was in. I was getting tired

standing by the fire, trying to get warm, when I noticed an empty rocker and thought it would be perfect by the fire. Before carrying it to the hearth, I reviewed in my head the difficulties of changing its location and decided that because Blue Mountain Center is a place where residents' happiness and comfort are paramount, everything would be fine. So, taking the few steps toward the inviting rocker, I announced my plan.

"No!" snapped Ben.

"No?" I queried

"The rockers are not allowed on the stone. You can take another chair." And right away, Jim got up and carried a chair to the hearth for me. The conversation we were all having about the world's troubles buzzed by me as I thought about the difference between cohousing and an artists' colony. Finally, I knew: The difference between cohousing and Blue Mountain Center, or most other places in this world, is that in cohousing communities, there is no Ben; no one who can say no and have the authority to make it stick.

Sometimes cohousing is compared to and sometimes it is confused with other types of intentional communities, with the communes of the sixties or with Brook Farm, the Transcendentalists' experiment in communal living in West Roxbury, Massachusetts, during the 1840s that Margaret Fuller and Nathaniel Hawthorne and a few other notables joined for a time. However, unlike most intentional communities that begin with a strong leader or with a guiding moral or religious code, there are no leaders, no formal directors, no staff, no rulers, no bosses, no ministers at Cambridge Cohousing or at any other cohousing community that I know of. In some ways, it is like a group of friends who are all equal and who all take turns organizing the next group activity, whether it is a dinner party or a night out. Norms of reciprocity keep things going among friends. They operate on what Lewis Hyde has called the "gift relationship" (Hyde 1979). If you invite me to dinner, I will feel a bit uncomfortable until I invite you to dinner. Friendship groups work because they are small, they don't have a great variety of activities, and they generally focus on enjoyable but not essential aspects of life.

If the analogy between cohousing and a friendship group doesn't fit, the more frequently mentioned correspondence with a large extended family is even less apt. Without a mother, a father, or other roles with culturally developed responsibilities and power, no one has obligations of obedience and no one has the power of authority. Lacking a leader, we soon learned that at Cambridge Cohousing, as at other cohousing communities, nothing happens unless one of us, or a group of us, makes it happen. Often, during our first fifteen years, attempts to make something happen were thwarted by the red card veto.

In those early days, and even today, many among us held the general misconception that commons manage themselves. That was Hardin's assumption when he argued in his extremely influential article that every commons was doomed to a tragic end (Hardin, 1968). Later, he indicated that he should have titled his essay "The Tragedy of the Unmanaged Commons" instead of just "The Tragedy of the Commons," and a half century later, Lewis Hyde, writing about how our cultural commons was being enclosed by extended copyright laws, suggested an even better title for Hardin's influential essay: "The Tragedy of the Unmanaged, Laissez-Faire, Common-Pool Resources with Easy Access for Noncommunicating, Self-Interested Individuals" (Hyde 2010, 44). Hyde drew partly on Ostrom's findings from her study of hundreds of long-lived commons (Ostrom 2015). Just as with any human group, commons need to be governed, managed in some way by communicating and cooperating participants. Ostrom developed eight principles for governing a commons:

- Define clear group boundaries.
- Match rules governing use of common goods to local needs and conditions.

- Ensure that those affected by the rules can participate in modifying the rules.
- Make sure the rule-making rights of community members are respected by outside authorities.
- Develop a system, carried out by community members, for monitoring members' behavior.
- Use graduated sanctions for rule violators.
- Provide accessible, low-cost means for dispute resolution.
- Build responsibility for governing the common resource in nested tiers from the lowest level up to the entire interconnected system.

During our first years of living together, we worked at many of those principles without knowing of Ostrom's research. The boundaries of our community were clear, but because a major point in crafting cohousing communities is to carve out more common space for communal activities than there is in most contemporary Western neighborhoods, cohousing communities can spend a lot of time drawing visible and invisible boundaries between what is the individual's and what is the group's.

We settled the question of how much of the scant acre and a quarter that our forty-one families shared would be partitioned off for private gardens and what those partitions would look like. We struggled for years over private storage in our common storage room and in the common areas next to our front doors, eventually divvying up the common storage room into private spaces. We also needed to decide whether those moving out and selling their units owed anything to the community, and we came to consensus that they didn't. We worked out a smoking policy: If your neighbor's smoke enters your unit through leaks separating units, do you have to grin and breathe it, or can the community develop smoking rules that govern an individual's private unit? In 2004, we adopted a no smoking policy and a smoke-free environment. But we never did develop a system, carried out by community members, for monitoring members' behavior; nor did we develop a system of graduated sanctions for rule violators. Instead, our resale circle does what it can to make sure that those who join us know what will be expected of them.

We Adopt a New and More Organized Form of Governance

We did all this for almost two decades by using consensus and colored cards. But increasingly, members of the community complained about the way things were going. Not only did a large number of proposals get dumped because someone threatened to red-card them but, without a formal hierarchy, a few individuals took rules and their enforcement into their own hands, sometimes making up the rules along the way. One was Joan. When she thought someone was doing something they shouldn't be doing, she demanded that the person stop doing it, expressing this in terms that most people feared to disobey.

For example, one cold, damp winter's evening I was walking Cola, the German shepherd–size cola-colored pup I call my granddog because she belongs to my grandkids, who live across the river in Brookline. When they all go away for a few days, I often Cola-sit. On that dark night when I came in from the street by the East End driveway with Cola, I had gotten as far down the spine path as the end of the vegetable garden, when, coming toward me from the glade, I heard Joan say "Did your dog leave poop on the path?" Since I hadn't been down that way, I said, "No, I don't think so." Joan approached, and, in her big black down coat, she must have seemed to Cola like a huge and scary figure coming out of the dark from nowhere. Cola, who is easily spooked, jumped back and jerked the leash, so that I was pulled slightly off balance.

"Oh, you mustn't do that," said Joan to Cola. "Diane is old and you have to be very careful not to jump like that and make her fall."

I was stunned. Joan often taunted me over the eight years I have on her, but talking to my dog about me with me standing right there, as some people do to children or patients, treating them as nonentities, was more disparaging than even Joan usually is. Regaining some composure, I said, "Where is the poop, Joan?" and Joan said to me, not to Cola this time, "Right in the middle of the path." I walked on and Joan warned, "Watch out, you'll step right in it." I looked down and there it was, a dark little pile about the size and shape of a miniature cinnamon bun. Joan had come up behind me and was looking over my shoulder. "A small dog left that," I said, and walked on toward the common house while Joan went to knock on Harriet and Paul's door. They had two King Charles spaniels.

I thought then about how different things must seem to Joan than they do to me. She has no difficulty reprimanding others and telling them how they should behave. She could march off to Paul's door and tell him to pick up the mess his dog left, without a shadow of a doubt that she was doing what she should be doing. I guess that is one reason Joan and David have always been against rules. Who needs to go to the trouble of coming to consensus on rules when you can decide all by yourself what other people should be doing and then quite easily and firmly tell them to do it, correcting them when you think they have transgressed? Our commons, being without an authority structure, had become a fertile field for freelance rulers (Freeman 1970).

Then in 2013, that began to change. If it takes a burning soul to bring a cohousing community to life, it also takes a burning soul or several of them working in concert to bring changes to a living community. For fifteen years, there was a lot of grousing about the overwhelming power of a few, but no one was doing anything about it. Then in 2013, Maria, Carla, and Viv started a study group to learn about something called sociocracy, a form of governance first suggested in the nineteenth century by Auguste Comte, the father of sociology, and refined over the years by many others. By 2013, there were a few consultants and guidebooks on sociocracy, and it was also being called "dynamic governance." Several other cohousing communities had given up on consensus in favor of sociocracy, and Jerry Koch Gonzales, who lived in Pioneer Valley Cohousing, a community in central Massachusetts that was an early adopter of sociocracy, was running workshops. He became our consultant and guide.

The study group kept at it and, with Jerry's help, its members developed a proposal to switch from our consensus government to dynamic governance and presented their idea to the community. At its November 2015 general meeting, the community agreed to try dynamic governance (DG) for six months (Buck and Villines 2019).

The proposal was detailed and brought extensive changes. Our loose committee structure was reorganized into a system of governing circles. As always, there would still be a general meeting once a month and that would be called a Full Circle Meeting. The managing board, which had responsibilities similar to managing boards of ordinary condos, would become the Condo Management Circle. Other committees were reorganized into three circles, based on what DG calls "domains," areas of responsibility. There would be the Outdoor Living Circle, which had responsibility for our outdoor property; the Extended Home Circle, which had responsibility for our indoor property, especially our common house; and the Community Connections Circle, which was actually a collection of subcircles that had responsibilities for events, communications (our Listserv and bulletin boards), meeting facilitation, and conflict resolution. One of the first tasks assigned to each of these circles was to establish its "aim"—its projects or goals and how it would work to serve the community.

Probably the most important change was the end of the colored-card system. The red card veto was gone and in its place was a formal decision-making process, with an opportunity for members to comment and voice objections to a proposal at every stage of its development. Objections to a proposal could no longer be personal ("I don't like it"). An objection had to be "paramount" and "argued," which meant that the objector had to explain why, if the proposal were adopted, it would be bad for the community. Following the trial period, the community set up a working circle called the Governance Development Circle (GDC) to study our new system, revise it, and produce a governing document.

This new governance system did not solve all of the community's problems. We still are not able to meet Ostrom's fifth and sixth system requirements: We have not developed a system, carried out by community members, for monitoring members' behavior, and we have not developed graduated sanctions for rule violators. But DG did help us travel the long road toward more efficient meetings, working groups (or circles) with the power to make decisions for their domains, and we do have sets of published rules lodged in documents rather than in the minds of powerful individuals. We are becoming a commonwealth of laws rather than a tyranny ruled by the divine right of personality.

We Were Becoming a NORC, Then Hope Arrived

One thing no amount of reorganization or democratic governance can accomplish is a membership that does not age. By 2020, two-thirds of those who had come together to form our community were still with us—empty-nesting and aging in place. Our stability is a measure of our success, but our stability is also the reason that by 2015 we were no longer a multigenerational community.

When we set out in the 1990s, we worked hard to meet our goal of filling our forty-one units so that one-third of them would house families with at least one child under thirteen. The other two-thirds were split between singles and any group of two or more adults. Back then, someone may have wondered what would happen as we all grew older, but, as far as I know, we never discussed what we would do to continue being an intergenerational community as our kids grew up and the rest of us grew older. So it was that when the last family with young children moved away in 2015, we had become what is sometimes referred to as a NORC, a naturally occurring retirement community, and it looked as though we would remain one as even our largest town houses became homes to a single person or an older couple.

We watched helplessly as Harriet and Paul, suffering unresolved anger with the rest of the community, put their large town house on the market with a realtor who knew nothing about cohousing and thought the community was an impediment to possible sales. There was a glimmer of hope as a couple with young children showed some interest in the unit, but it came to nothing amid rumors that someone told them that our community was not friendly toward kids. In the end, it sold to a middle-aged couple who had never heard of cohousing and had no wish to be part of a community. Not long after, a set of moves and unit exchanges left the West End without the one young family it had housed.

For years, the jungle gym on our pretty good lawn stood empty, a monument to our intergenerational aspirations. There was even a move afoot by those ready to accept our fate to remove the indoor kiddie slide and turn the children's room where it stood into a quiet dining room. (We still hadn't solved the noise problem in our dining room and, with more and more of us needing hearing aids, meals were becoming rarer and more sparsely attended.) Then luck struck.

As is always the case in cohousing communities, nothing happens unless there is at least one burning soul working hard to make it happen. Without any of us knowing about it, without our burning soul herself knowing about it, sparks were igniting. Hope, our burning soul, and her husband, Ezra, had moved to North Cambridge after college. They often walked by the CAMBRIDGE COHOUSING sign at our entranceway and wondered about cohousing. Then, by chance, they took a course with a couple who had sublet a unit at Cambridge Cohousing, and as they walked home with them after class, they would pass our sign and start talking about our community. According to Hope, the couple was "just so enthusiastic about what a warm and welcoming community it was."

In 2016, Hope and Ezra's son, Jules, was born and they came to an open house for a small town house in the West End that was on the market. For many reasons, they were primed to like it: The unit was small but sufficient. ("We use every square inch of the place, which we really like from an eco-perspective; it controls us so we are not too acquisitive of extra stuff, 'cause we don't have space.") They had been looking for community for quite a while. ("Even though we hadn't heard about cohousing, before knowing this cohousing, we had always searched for a more communal spirit with neighbors and had never achieved it. . . . You don't pick your neighbors, and most Americans are not very comfortable with cold calling.") And it was getting difficult for Hope to carry Jules up to their steep third-floor walk-up.

Once they had moved into CCH, Hope and Ezra worried about being the only family with a young child in the community, but they decided that Hope would get on the resale and marketing committee and try to bring other young families in. ("We knew we were taking a leap of faith. . . . We didn't want to live in a community only with elders. We . . . knew that this was a dream come true for any parent of young kids; it's gotta be possible to get other young families to take the plunge . . . and by virtue of being a young person with young kids, I can be a more convincing salesperson for other families with young kids.")

The first opportunity came when a couple with a son the same age as Jules needed to make a quick move from California at the same time that a large unit in the common house came on the market. Hope talked to the other mother on the phone and emails flew back and forth. "I think I was helpful," said Hope, "because she could ask young mother things of me and she had the sense that she would have at least one other peer here."

When the couple from California moved in, we had two young families, each with a three-year-old boy. The next unit to go on the market was a large town house. By that time, Hope had gotten the resale and marketing committee geared up to attract young families. When the large town house went up for sale, she got young families to come to open houses by "plastering flyers in playgrounds and other places that young families go to." Then at the open houses, she started in our dining room with the two children's playrooms next door. She spent "a lot of time talking about everything that was amazing about this place for parenting. Then it kind of sells itself." She showed them all of our facilities, the library and the rec room with its pool table and Ping-Pong table and pointed out how great they would be for older kids. For younger kids, she pointed to our large yard with its jungle gym, noting that "nobody could afford a huge yard like this in Cambridge for themselves . . . you'd have to move out to the suburbs for that." But even more than the facilities, Hope was able to talk about "the community itself and the idea of the weekly meals and just having neighbors that we know." She was able to push the "idea of having a village to help raise the kids, and it was really easy to talk up just how welcoming everybody has been and being able to let Jules just run and not worry about it." She talked about our ecofriendliness and was careful to reassure people "that even though it's a community on the older side . . . it *is* very welcoming, and desperate for kids. . . . A lot of people would ask me things like 'Won't people be mad at me and yell if the kids are making noise?' and I'd say, 'No.'"

Hope was able to give the example of what happened when a few of the older members worried about the kids racing their trikes up and down the spine. A few people got together to make stop signs and talked to the kids about traffic rules. "It wasn't at all an antagonistic process; it was just a very community-oriented process and supportive of the kids learning boundaries that are appropriate—'No, don't go too fast on your bike when you're on the sidewalk with other people.' That's a good life lesson."

Describing her approach to potential buyers, Hope said, "So many of us have had experiences in the broader world of having older people yell at us for the way our kids are behaving. That just happens a lot. People aren't that tolerant. . . . People will say things like 'Mind your children,' and it's just not nice. I think some of what I was able to do that was probably harder for the marketing and resale committee to do before me, I was able to speak from experience and say, 'No, these elders are kind and loving toward children and they understand and they really want children to be part of the community, so they are willing to work with the parents.'"

Hope was so convincing that two young families bid for the large town house. It sold to a family with another three-year-old boy and a younger daughter. At that point, we had three young families. Then Harriet and Paul's large town house went on the market again and the three young couples who were already here were able to tell their friends about it. As Hope said, "This was where we started to get a little bit of a network effect, because all of the current young families sent out the notices to our preschool and school cohort of parents." As it happened, one of their friends from preschool had just moved to Belmont, a suburban community close to Cambridge. Margaret was a stay-at-home mom and Phil worked long hours, which became even longer when his office moved and his commute doubled. Margaret said she felt isolated in Belmont and was eager to have friends to talk to and other kids for her kids to play with. So, even though it meant moving twice in less than a year, they sprang for it.

After that, a one-bedroom unit went on the market. Jan, a single mom with a young daughter, had wanted to move to Cambridge

Cohousing, but the units were either too big or too small, and once again, the one-bedroom unit was too small. So Marcia, who lived alone, offered to trade units—she'd let Jan have her small two-bedroom unit and she took the large one-bedroom one that was on the market. After that, one more sale, this time of a very small one-bedroom unit, brought a young couple, and so we had six young families, with eight kids under five.

In less than five years, we had turned from a NORC back into a multigenerational community. I asked Hope how she thought the community might have to change to accommodate all of these new young families, and she said, "I don't think we need to change things now. . . . I personally don't feel super rushed to get to the point where it's back to one- third, one-third, one-third ratio, because it already feels like there's a cohort of kids and they're the right ages with each other and they like each other."

Hope and Ezra had another baby, the first baby in the community in more than a decade, and Hope said, "I'm going to be able to be even more of a convincing spokesperson now because it's been so amazing to be able to have so many different people offer to hold her, and just comparing my maternity leave with Jules to my maternity leave with her, it was so much nicer with her. . . . It was a real blessing to be able to come to common meals here with the little baby and be able to pass her around and get some social outlets, even though I was still just at home. And during the day, being able to have people come over and hold her for an hour and get a nap in. Lori came over and gave me a foot rub; it was just so nice."

Hope noted that Margaret was already helping on the meals committee and added, "I know there had been debates to repurpose the playrooms because they hadn't been used so much, but that would have been a lot harder to get us here if there hadn't been those playrooms. That's just a physical amenity, but it's a sign of the community being oriented in a friendly way. . . . That was a very funny part of the early months here. People just coming and saying, 'Hold your ground. Say that you need to keep that slide.' So we felt very supported from day one. . . . I feel the difference. It feels different than when we first moved in. It feels better. It's lots of things working together, but I think you did need that spark."

• • •

A lot has changed since I began looking for a cohousing community in 1993. There are now over three hundred forming and built cohousing communities in the United States; Cambridge Cohousing is more than two decades old; and my four grandchildren were born and grew up during this time period. The youngest graduated from college in 2021, but there was no pomp and circumstance for him. To stop COVID-19, we are cautioned to keep six feet from all but our housemates. Unfortunately, for all of us, cohousers and everybody else, those housemates have become fewer over the years. We live in ever smaller households. Close to a third of Americans now live alone. In one sense, that is a measure of our affluence. We live alone because we can afford to live alone and, although most of us might like more companionship, we prefer our solitary quarters to any housemate we can think of—and maybe any possible housemate prefers solitary quarters to us. Only on Zoom do we get together with family and friends; but there our solitary existence is rendered in stark relief as we peer from our single-headed screen tiles to their multiheaded tiles. Thusly does the coronavirus pandemic exacerbate the loneliness epidemic.

"We're all in this together," the catchphrase of the pandemic, gives a nod to the commons, but the unemployed, the poor, and the single know it's not true. When we check the pandemic's progress by focusing on infections and deaths per hundred worldwide, by nation, by state, and by city, it does look as though we are seeing the pandemic through the lens of a commons. Unfortunately, when we scroll down to deaths by region, race, or income, we discover a virus that attacks those who were vulnerable before the pandemic hit. We are not all in this together and that is one reason why the virus is getting the better of us. Our individual ability to fend off the viral attack depends on our position and condition before the virus leaped from some other species to ours, and that depends on class and race as much as on anything an individual does. If we were middle-class, had a college degree, and were part of a favored race and ethnicity when the virus struck, our chances of getting through this pandemic alive and well are pretty good. If on the other hand, we were hungry when the virus struck, we were more likely to be victims. At the same time that poverty has been declining, economic inequality has been increasing.

Nonetheless, in the balance between the market and the commons, the virus has forced us to recognize the commons to a degree that we haven't since King John signed the Magna Carta in 1215. Time will let us know whether the virus's attack will rouse our sense that we really are in this together or whether in a year or so, once the epidemic is over, we will return to a status quo ante and the trend lines of our inequality, a measure denoting the sickness of our commons, will continue the upward march begun in the seventies.

Here at Cambridge Cohousing, our new dynamic governance methods made it quite easy to quickly muster a response to the virus. Shortly after Governor Baker issued his social-distancing orders, our managing board appointed a COVID-19 team, which drew up rules for our community. We closed down all of our common spaces except the children's rooms and the laundry room—no more exercise room, no meals together, no concerts or other events. We limited the laundry room to common house residents—one at a time—and we ran washers once a day with a half a cup of bleach and wiped the button panels on the machines when we finished. No more visitors. Only residents could use our lobbies and our elevator, except for caregivers, common-area cleaners, and emergency workers. Our many meetings were held by Zoom, even if the others in our circle were only two doors down the hall. Some of us were assigned to go around every couple of hours to wipe down and disinfect high-touch surfaces such as door handles, entry keypads, and light switches.

At the same time that we closed down most of the facilities and activities that we enjoyed, we added a host of other activities to ease the pain. Beyond our borders, the public playgrounds and child-care centers were wrapped in yellow caution tape, but our kids had our jungle gym, and they could race their bikes from the east end to the west end, yelling all the way. On our Listserv, we shared a regular flow of forwarded texts about the virus—including a quick correction if anybody forwarded a flawed text. There was also a list of the local stores that had toilet paper in stock and another list of the stores that made deliveries. Maybe even more useful was the daily dose of jokes and music.

Some of us were watching the Met's free streaming operas and talking about each performance at our daily cocktail hour the next day if the sun was out and we could gather on our patio, which was not often that spring on the East Coast. We participated in the neighborhood teddy bear hunt, and many first- and second-floor windows displayed a big bear. A few of us let everyone know when we were going to a store and offered to pick up orders for everyone else. A team got busy sewing face masks for everyone else and for area hospitals—they sent out an appeal for materials, especially wire and elastic. All of the singles—about half of us—chose a buddy to be our link to the world in case the virus found our lungs.

During the first year, the virus only reached one household. We got daily updates from that household and from Olga, who has a friend who was visiting family in NYC and came back infected. In the second week, she reported that her friend had been released from the hospital and was back at home, but he had suffered heart and lung damage. That's how we learned about residual damage.

Larry turned four. He was sad that he couldn't have a regular party, but his mom planned an alternative party: We all dressed up in costumes and sang to him on the pretty great lawn. Then he rode his bike to the east end, where we took many photos and sang to him again. The kids did not stay six feet apart. How can you explain a virus to a four-year-old? Our new baby began to teethe, and we wondered what she was thinking as she looked out at a world of masked admirers. The best part of our new young family cohort was that for the school year, from fall 2020 till spring 2021, the parents got together and hired two teachers so that our kids could take over the dining room and the rec room and we could run our own school.

* * *

Cohousing works. It works for Hope, who wants to be living in a village with elders to hold her infant while she naps, and it works for me, who loves to hold her infant. But I still miss the nonstop conversation I enjoyed with Dick, and when I Zoom with family or with other cohousers, I look from my single-headed screen tile and I am envious as all get-out of my married neighbors in their multiheaded tiles. They have cohousing and each other—a double shield against loneliness. As Peter said, "It's only cohousing."

As long as we burn coal and oil, the doomsday clock will tick. As long as the couple is the only strong and enduring social connection, loneliness will continue its march toward pandemic proportions. But those who find their cohousing community do have a defense against the crushing pain of loneliness. It's only cohousing, but the more it helps us to think like commoners rather than marketers, the more we'll be able to be a force to save ourselves and our planet.

Bibliography

Allcot, Dawn. 2021. "5 Mind-Blowing Facts About Jeff Bezos' Wealth." July 27, 2021. https://www.yahoo.com/now/5-mind -blowing-facts-jeff-182204262.html.

Bass, Alison. 1991. "Welcome Home." *Boston Globe Magazine*, August 11, 1991.

Beasley, David. 2020. "The Nobel Peace Prize 2020, World Food Pro-gramme (WFP) Acceptance Speech." https://www.nobelprize.org /prizes/peace/2020/wfp/acceptance-speech/

Bellamy, Edward. 2009. *Looking Backward 2000–1887*. Edited by Mat-thew Beaumont. Oxford: Oxford University Press.

Berners-Lee, Tim. 2000. *Weaving the Web: The Original Design and Ultimate Destiny of the World Wide Web*. San Francisco: Harper Business.

Bollier, David. 2014. *Think Like a Commoner: A Short Introduction to the Life of the Commons*. Gabriola Island, BC: New Society Publishers.

Boyer, Robert H. W., and Suzanne Leland. 2018. "Cohousing for Whom? Survey Evidence to Support the Diffusion of Socially and Spatially Integrated Housing in the United States." *Housing Policy*

Debate 28, no. 5: 653–67. https://doi.org/10.1080/10511482
.2018.1424724.

Boyle, James. 2003. "The Second Enclosure Movement and the Construction of the Public Domain." *Law and Contemporary Problems*
66, no. 1/2 (Winter/Spring): 33–74.

Brown, Patricia Leigh. 1998. "Honk If You Like Ecological Housing."
New York Times, April 16, 1998.

Buck, John, and Sharon Villines. 2019. *We the People: Consenting to a
Deeper Democracy: A Handbook for Understanding and Implementing
Sociocratic Principles and Practices.* 2d ed. Washington, DC:
Sociocracy.info.

Butler, Lawrence C.T., and Amy Rothstein. 1991. *On Conflict and
Consensus: A Handbook on Formal Consensus Decisionmaking.*
Tacoma Park, MD: Food Not Bombs Publishing.

Chiodelli, Francesco. 2015. "What Is Really Different Between
Cohousing and Gated Communities?" *European Planning Studies*
23, no. 12: 2566–81. https://doi.org/10.1080/09654313.2015
.1096915.

Coolidge, Calvin. "Calvin Coolidge Quotes." BrainyQuote. Accessed
October 16, 2021. https://www.brainyquote.com/authors/
calvin-coolidge-quotes.

Didion, Joan. 2005. *The Year of Magical Thinking.* New York: Knopf.

Erikson, Kai. 1976. *Everything in Its Path.* New York: Simon & Schuster.
https://www.simonandschuster.com/books/Everything-in-its
-Path/Kai-T-Erikson/9780671240677.

Freeman, Jo. 1970. "The Tyranny of Stuctureless." https://www
.jofreeman.com/joreen/tyranny.htm.

Giese, Jo. 1990. "A Communal Type of Life and Dinners for Everyone." *New York Times,* September 27, 1990.

Goodman, Percival, and Paul Goodman. 1990. *Communitas: Means of
Livelihood and Ways of Life.* New York: Columbia University Press.

Graae, Bodil. 1967. "Children Should Have One Hundred Parents."
Politiken, April 1967.

Gudmand-Høyer, Jan. 1968. "The Missing Link Between Utopia and the Dated One-Family House." This article was originally published in Danish.

Hardin, Garrett. 1968. "The Tragedy of the Commons." *Science, New Series* 162, no. 3859: 1243–48.

Hayden, Dolores. 2002. *Redesigning the American Dream: The Future of Housing, Work and Family Life.* 2d ed. New York: W. W. Norton.

Homewood Friends. 2015. "Introduction to Quaker Worship." *Homewood Friends Meeting* (blog). February 18, 2015. https://homewood friends.org/2015/02/17/introduction-to-quaker-worship-2/.

Hyde, Lewis. 1979. *The Gift: Imagination and the Erotic Life of Property.* New York: Vintage.

———. 2010. *Common as Air: Revolution, Art, and Ownership.* New York: Farrar, Straus and Giroux.

Kipling, Rudyard. 1886. *Departmental Ditties and Other Verses.* https://www.telelib.com/authors/K/KiplingRudyard/verse/Depatmental Ditties/index.html.

Knapp, Caroline. 1999. *Pack of Two: The Intricate Bond Between People and Dogs.* New York: Dial Press.

Kübler-Ross, Elizabeth, and David Kessler. 2005. *On Grief and Grieving: Finding the Meaning of Grief Through the Five Stages of Loss.* New York: Scribner.

Lazar, Peter. 2006. *Cohousing Blog* (blog). August 23, 2006.

Lewis, C. S. 2001. *A Grief Observed.* San Francisco: HarperOne. https://www.christianbook.com/a-grief-observed-c-s-lewis /9780060652388/pd/52381.

McCamant, Kathryn, and Charles Durrett. 1988. *Cohousing: A Contemporary Approach to Housing Ourselves.* Berkeley: Ten Speed Press. 2011. *Creating Cohousing: Building Sustainable Communities.* Gabriola Island, BC: New Society Publishers.

Munoz, Ana Patricia at al. 2015. "The Color of Wealth in Boston." SSRN Scholarly Paper ID 2630261. Rochester, NY: Social Science Research Network. https://doi.org/10.2139/ssrn.2630261.

Ostrom, Elinor. 2015. *Governing the Commons: The Evolution of Institutions for Collective Action.* Cambridge: Cambridge University Press. https://doi.org/10.1017/CBO9781316423936.

Putnam, Robert D. 2000. *Bowling Alone: The Collapse and Revival of American Community.* New York: Simon & Schuster.

Robert, Henry M. 1967. *Robert's Rules of Order.* Edited by Rachel Vixman. New York: Pyramid Books.

Roiphe, Anne Richardson. 2008. *Epilogue: A Memoir.* New York: HarperCollins.

Rose, Carol. 2003. "Romans, Roads, and Romantic Creators." *Law and Contemporary Problems* 66, no. 1/2 (Winter/Spring): 89–110.

Rowe, Jonathan. 2013. *Our Common Wealth: The Hidden Economy That Makes Everything Else Work.* San Francisco: Berrett-Koehler Publishers.

Ruiu, Maria L. 2014. "Differences Between Cohousing and Gated Communities: A Literature Review." *Sociological Inquiry* 84, no. 2: 316–35. https://doi.org/10.1111/soin.12031.

Sahlins, Marshall, and David Graeber. 2017. *Stone Age Economics.* London and New York: Routledge.

Steenland, Sally. 2013. "Resolve to End Homelessness in 2013." Center for American Progress, January 2, 2013.

Acknowledgments

A project as complex as this book depended on many helping hands. My most essential and heartfelt thanks go to my fellow cohousers. They have sustained me, cheered me, and nurtured me through many years. They are my subjects and my support. For the sake of their privacy, I have changed their names in the text, but most will probably recognize themselves and each other. A few fellow cohousers read early drafts and made helpful and critical suggestions. These included Eva Kassel, Carol Kunik, and Ileana Jones.

I first learned about cohousing from Harriet Barlow while gardening with her at Blue Mountain Center in the Adirondacks. She, BMC, and its current director, Ben Strader, offered me a place to write at various stages as this manuscript grew from daily notetaking through its many drafts. Before I started taking notes in earnest, however, I told my friends stories about my new project. At dinner one evening my good friend and colleague, Jane Martin, listened and said, "that's your next book." That's when I started taking careful and complete notes. About halfway through, I discovered Elinor Ostrom and the commons; I finally knew what I was writing about. In 2011, David Entin and I formed an organization to study cohousing. We called it the Cohousing Research Network. Members of its steering committee have been very helpful: Angela Sanguinetti, Chuck MacLane, Neil Planchon, and Heidi Berggren. Friends and relatives read the developing drafts: William Scott Long, Vinz Muser, and grandchildren Isabel, Maya, Anna, and Jeremy. They suggested that I be more positive and focus on our successes rather than our challenges. My son Philip read an early draft and guided me well; my son, Harry, read a later draft with care, pointing out needed changes.

Help to find, choose, and use the photographs came from several quarters: Jean Mason helped me find her husband Ed's photographs, and their daughter, Andrea Nolan, put them into usable shape. Cambridge Cohousing is blessed with many fine photographers. Chief among them is Richard Curran who chronicles our events. Most of the photographs from our website are his. Mark Ostow helped when he had a moment and taught me what little I know about recognizing a good photograph.

The manuscript benefited from two editors at New Village Press, Kat Corfman and Grace Woodruff. Of course, my greatest thanks go to Lynne Elizabeth at New Village who saw the value of this book and shepherded me and the book to its conclusion. I am also grateful to Gwen Noyes and Art Klipfel whose hard work helped to turn our dreams into our homes. Although in the balance between the market and the commons I often saw them leaning toward the market, their work did produce the structure within which a commons came to life along with the home in which I now live. At the last moment, when the book was almost ready to go to press, old friend and colleague of my husband and our sons, Ken Coughlin, stepped in to help proofread.

Each of these guides and friends helped me to make this a better book. Its flaws are mine alone.

About the Author

Diane Rothbard Margolis is a founding member of Cambridge Cohousing where she has lived for more than twenty years. She is a former member of the Coho/US Board of Directors and co-founder and Director Emeritus of the Co-housing Research Network. She was a fellow at the Radcliffe Institute for Advanced Study 1980–1981.
She has published many research articles, and her books include *The Fabric of Self,* which won Honorable Mention at the First Annual Book Award of the Eastern Sociological Society. She is Professor Emerita of Sociology at the University of Connecticut.

CPSIA information can be obtained
at www.ICGtesting.com
Printed in the USA
JSHW022043221022
31947JS00001B/1

9 781613 321782